Praise for *Momentun*

"What is it about Michael Slaughter? How does he always 'get it?' Every time I read something by Michael, I think, 'Why didn't I think of that?' He is always a step ahead of most of us. His thinking is adequately 'fermented' by time, expertise and practical application. His writing is 'content rich.' It is never 'cotton candy' material. It is profoundly high protein. Here is the rule of thumb: anything by Michael Slaughter is definitely worth reading—including this one!"

Dr. Jim Garlow
Senior Pastor, Skyline Wesleyan Church
San Diego, CA

"For too long the importance of the inner life of the leader has been ignored. But not so with Michael Slaughter's book *Momentum for Life*. From personal experience he shares the truth that you can't give what you don't have. Mike gives us a no compromise spiritual diet for being ALL the leader God has called us to be."

Bill Easum
author of *Put On Your Own Oxygen Mask First*
www.easumbandy.com

"Not only does Mike Slaughter speak convincingly to the pressing issues of our daily lives, he provides helpful direction for us to wrestle with these issues."

Dr. Maxie Dunnam
Chancellor, Asbury Theological Seminary

"Michael Slaughter sounds a clarion call to leaders. He develops disciplines that we constantly adopt and observe in order to gain momentum and become stronger in our leadership effectiveness. He targets pitfalls to avoid and positive disciplines to practice. He is on target!"

Dr. John Ed Mathison
Senior Pastor, Frazer Memorial United Methodist Church
Montgomery, AL

Other Books
by Michael Slaughter

Spiritual Entrepreneurs: Six Principles for Risking Renewal (Abingdon Press, 1995)

Out on the Edge: A Wake-Up Call for Church Leaders on the Edge of the Media Reformation (Abingdon Press, 1998)

Real Followers: Beyond Virtual Christianity (Abingdon Press, 1999)

UnLearning Church: Transforming Spiritual Leadership for the Emerging Church (Group Publishing, 2002)

Momentum for Life

Momentum for Life

Sustaining Personal Health, Integrity, and Strategic Focus as a Leader

Michael Slaughter

with Warren Bird and Kim Miller

Abingdon Press
Nashville

MOMENTUM FOR LIFE:
SUSTAINING PERSONAL HEALTH, INTEGRITY, AND
STRATEGIC FOCUS AS A LEADER

Copyright © 2005 Michael Slaughter

All rights reserved.

This book is printed on recycled, acid-free paper.

Library of Congress Cataloging-in-Publication Data

Slaughter, Michael.
    Momentum for life : sustaining personal health, integrity, and strategic focus as a leader / Michael Slaughter with Warren Bird and Kim Miller.
        p. cm.
    ISBN 0-687-33191-9
    1. Leadership--Religious aspects--Christianity. 2. Christian leadership. 3. Leadership.   I. Bird, Warren. II. Miller, Kim, 1956-   . III. Title.
BV4597.53.L43S53 2005
253--dc22   2005018851

Cover design and photography by Brad Wise, Dayton, OH

05 06 07 08 09 10 11 12 13 14—10 09 08 07 06 05 04 03 02 01

To my nine Young Heroes—
Thomas Beechem, Matt Cermak,
Jon Crawford, Kelsey Francis,
Anna Mathias, Jason Meyer, Erica Prigg,
Jonathan Slaughter, and
Ann Marie Wainscott
—who are running the race of faith with
the passion and endurance to win.

Contents

1. Momentum: Mass in Motion **13**

2. **D**evotion to God **43**

3. **R**eadiness for Lifelong Learning **69**

4. **I**nvesting in Key Relationships **93**

5. **V**isioning for the Future **115**

6. **E**ating and Exercise for Life........................**143**

7. Work Your Program:
   Thriving in Life, Leadership, and Mission **163**

Appendix: Resources to Keep You Growing.......**171**

Acknowledgments

I am indebted to the great cloud of witnesses who have surrounded my life with models for living, many of whom are named in the pages of this book with specific examples of their impact. I especially want to thank my family: wife Carolyn, daughter and son-in-law Kristen and Brendan, and son Jonathan, who have embraced the disciplines of momentum for their lives as well. I give thanks for Pastor Wayne Cordeiro, New Hope Christian Fellowship O'ahu, who triggered the idea that led to Ginghamsburg's *Transformation Journal* mentioned throughout this book.

Kim Miller, creative director at Ginghamsburg, partners with me in worship design as well as book design and has tirelessly nurtured God's heartbeat for this work. She, along with the other members of Ginghamsburg's senior management team—Pastors Sue Nilson Kibbey and Mike Bowie, along with John Jung, Karen Smith, and Steve Swallow—support me in ways that enable me to put focus on what I do best at Ginghamsburg. Numerous support personnel also contributed to the creation of this book, including Todd Carter, Michael Pollard, Penny Powers, Brad Wise, Dwayne and Kay Ann Wilson, and the servants on Ginghamsburg's Internet team headed by Mark Stephenson.

Warren Bird, collaborative author and longtime friend, arranged my written outlines into flowing paragraphs, filled in missing pieces, and offered valuable content suggestions.

The dedication page of this book credits a rising generation. Their momentum for life exceeds my own, and God will do far greater things through them as a result.

CHAPTER ONE

Momentum: Mass in Motion

MOMENTUM> *Mass in motion. Quantity of forward motion. Impetus. i.e.: "A team that has momentum is on the move and hard to stop."*

"I rejoiced with those who said to me, 'Let us go to the house of the LORD.'" (Ps. 122:1)

The World Series, even though it's an annual fall classic, rarely captures my attention. Most years you have to remind me who won by the beginning of spring training just four months later.

Don't get me wrong. I am a lifelong baseball enthusiast. All the boys I knew while growing up in Cincinnati in the 1950s and '60s were baptized in sauerkraut, German beer, and baseball. A trip with my dad to old Crosley Field to see young Frank Robinson send one downtown was truly a transcendental experience.

There is only one problem with the World Series. Most years my hometown team is not in it, so come October my attention turns to more pressing matters.

There was something different about the series of 2004, however. The Boston Red Sox had a history of coming up one short. They had not won a series since 1918, after which they traded Babe Ruth to the New York Yankees. Between 1918 and 2003, the Sox appeared in only four World Series, losing each in game seven. Their almost-victory in 1986 found them one out away from a long-awaited championship, only to be denied as history watched the ball roll through first baseman Bill Buckner's legs and out to right field. He didn't get his glove low enough, the ball escaped, and the Mets scored the series-winning run.

The curse of the Bambino (as people called it) struck again in 2004 as the Sox fell to the mighty Yankees in the first three games of the American League playoffs. No team had ever come back after being down three games to none. Boston would need to win four games straight, the last two of them in Yankee Stadium.

The Red Sox won games four and five, and then I turned my TV back on. There was a growing confidence in the eyes of the players as they traveled to New York for the sixth game of the series. It appeared that momentum had begun to turn in their direction. A team that has momentum is on the move and hard to stop.

A team that has momentum is on the move and hard to stop.

Boston went on to accomplish what no other team in the history of baseball has ever done. They won the championship series against the Yankees after being down three games to none, and then swept the St. Louis Cardinals in four straight games to win the World Series.

Momentum for Life

Every baseball team goes into the season with the goal to get to the Series and win the prize. Some teams break out early in the season only to fade in the heat of August. Others patiently persist, paying the daily dues of disciplined practice on the fundamentals.

You cannot get to where you want to be in your faith, influence, relationships, vocation, or physical-emotional health if you are not moving forward.

Likewise, you cannot get where you want to be in your faith, influence, relationships, vocation, or physical-emotional health if you are

14

not moving forward. From presidents to priests, the landscape is cluttered with the corpses of talented leaders who failed to keep the positive momentum of character development.

All leadership begins with self-leadership.

The media shouts "leadership failure" on a daily basis. Leaders have failed all around us, from the military command at Abu Ghraib prison to the *USA Today* plagiarism scandal. From Bill Clinton's indiscretions to Martha Stewart's deceptions, from the executive failure at Enron to the high-tech meltdown—government, business, and religious leaders alike stumble into the oblivion of moral and ethical failure.

Many church problems trace back to a failure of leadership as well. They show up in the Catholic sex-abuse scandal and its widespread cover-up. They're evident when the president of a major Protestant denomination admits to an extra-marital affair and is jailed for financial misdealing. Maintaining life-momentum is imperative if you are going to faithfully navigate your way through a world of clouded moral boundaries.

Maintaining life-momentum is imperative if you are going to faithfully navigate your way through a world of clouded moral boundaries.

It is one thing to aspire to run the race of influential leadership but quite another to faithfully finish it. The spirit of any movement or organization is created from the top. A fish begins to rot at the head.

While I was working on this chapter, Dan Rather announced that he would soon step down as anchor of *CBS Evening News*. My morning newspaper recalled the damning independent review of the false report given on the program *60 Minutes* concerning President George W. Bush's National Guard service. The failure to follow the disciplined procedures of faithful reporting resulted in the firing of three news executives and a producer. The incident no doubt also influenced the timing of Dan Rather's announcement. Not exactly the footnote that you want on your obituary after a long, illustrious career! All leadership begins with self-leadership.

All leadership begins with self-leadership.

Settling for Lesser Dreams

We dream about the incredible opportunities that we have as leaders to influence the world for God's purpose. Through God's Spirit, we can make a lasting contribution that benefits the well-being of others. But having a *dream* and having the disciplined lifelong commitment to *realize that dream* are two different things. It is easy to make a commitment, but keeping that commitment for life is another matter.

When I was in seminary, I hung out with five guys. We were drawn to each other because in our pre-Christian lives all of us had lived large and lived lost. Each of us had known some form of major failure, and then experienced a radical transformation in Jesus Christ. All had passion to be used by God in major ways. All of us were married, and voiced our commitment to make our marriages last a lifetime.

> **I see the temptation in bright, rising stars is to compromise their idealistic visions by age thirty, working for money instead of meaning.**

Things haven't turned out the way we planned. Today only two of the five are still married to the same woman of our seminary days. Of those two, both endured years of marital crisis, which we survived only by God's grace.

Over the course of life, most good things don't happen magically or suddenly. They are the result of a predetermined desire, an ongoing commitment to build momentum for life. Faith is not an instant realization of a desired future, for nothing worthwhile can be acquired at once.

> *Now faith is being sure of what we hope for and certain of what we do not see.* (Heb. 11:1)

Many young leaders start with dreams of walking closely with God and being used by God to make a difference on planet Earth. As I invest the second half of my life in training young leaders, however, I see the temptation in bright, rising stars to compromise their idealistic visions by age thirty. They begin to work for money instead of meaning. They settle for a job instead of a life calling. They make their life about personal achievement instead of focusing on making a lasting contribution.

Young people are selling out and old people are cashing out.

God wants so much more. God wants to build lifelong momentum toward what we were created to become. The apostle Paul compares the life of faith to running a race that requires the impetus of momentum.

> *Do you not know that in a race all the runners run, but only one gets the prize? Run in such a way as to get the prize. Everyone who competes in the games goes into strict training. They do it to get a crown that will not last; but we do it to get a crown that will last forever. Therefore I do not run like someone running aimlessly; I do not fight like a boxer beating the air. No, I strike a blow to my body and make it my slave so that after I have preached to others, I myself will not be disqualified for the prize.* (1 Cor. 9:24-27)

Instead of climbing to new heights, too many leaders plateau when they meet resistance. It doesn't have to be that way. God wants to win the battle for the soul of the world, and it begins with management of our own inner world. I've learned this the hard way through several conversion-like crises:

- *My marriage.* On June 1, 1992, my wife Carolyn and I made the disciplined commitment to start our marriage over. We had been married almost twenty years and were headed toward divorce. Instead, I had a conversion about investing in that key relationship.

- *My devotion.* On August 17, 1994, I traveled to Korea with a doctor of ministry class from a nearby seminary. As we learned first-hand about the amazing revival sweeping that country, I saw that the real power was in the Korean church's commitment to prayer. I made the disciplined commitment to begin every day with a time of devotional meditation and prayer.

- My *body*. On August 18, 2000, I was at a restaurant and started to feel sick. Seconds later I collapsed and was rushed to the hospital. In the days that followed, a cardiologist said I hadn't taken good care of my heart and body. My body fat content was in the 30s—a ridiculously high level. So in October 2000 I started working with a personal trainer. I was converted in the way I eat and exercise.

After all these events came together, I discovered a combination of life practices that enable me to build momentum for life and keep me on an upward climb. When any parts of this practice are neglected, I begin to plateau and lose momentum. Worse, I begin to downsize God's dream. Every follower of Christ needs to find the self-management practices that create momentum for life. Mine are based on the acronym D-R-I-V-E. They are the elements that keep me moving with momentum towards God's promised future.

Devotion

D stands for **d**evotion. Many church leaders lack depth and prophetic clarity because their devotional lives are superficial. The rigorous discipline of daily Bible study and journaling vitalizes my devotion to God. I do it first thing in the morning, just like I shave, shower, and dress for the day. If I don't practice this discipline, I find that it takes me only twenty-four hours to lose my fear of God.

Whatever I'm devoted to is who I become. I want to see life through God's eyes and to become passionate about the concerns that matter most to God.

There is a big difference between deciding what I want to do versus discerning what God is doing, and then moving to what God is blessing. My devotional practice is the S.O.N. method that helps me see through the eyes of the SON of God. It involves the **S**cripture I'll read for the day, journaling **O**bservations from what I read, and then **N**aming practical applications for my life. I then take time to express my feelings and thoughts in a written prayer. Later, I'll show you a specific example of what I do.

Readiness

R represents **r**eadiness for lifelong learning. I'm an avid reader and spend at least an hour a day reading about the best practices of leadership culture today as well as staying faithful to ancient truths of the past. As a disciple of Jesus (the word *disciple* means learner), I want everything I read and observe to impact the faithfulness and effectiveness of my life ascent. Jesus said, "My *sheep hear my voice*" (John 10:27, KJV), and I want to learn to better recognize his voice.

In chapter 3 we will look at the importance of having this disciplined practice of lifelong learning. I'll share with you my personal daily regime. What are you reading and learning? A lot of people lose the momentum of learning when the diploma is received. That's one reason people restlessly move from church to church, because the leader quits learning. He or she has grown redundant and boring, having nothing new to say.

Investing

I denotes investing in key relationships, beginning with my family. I've rearranged my work schedule so that my life partner Carolyn feels supported by me rather than widowed by the church. I'm committed to putting my family before my work and church.

I also invest in other people who are strategic for the mission. All people are equally important to God, but not all are equally strategic for the expenditure of your time for God's purpose.

All people are equally important to God, but not all are equally strategic for the expenditure of your time for God's purpose.

Maybe for you it's a key group of elders who act as unpaid staff. For me right now, it's the senior management team at Ginghamsburg Church. They are my "mission critical people," the only people besides my family who can contact me anytime, even when I'm on vacation.

Who is most strategic in *your* life? Too often we let others set and fill our schedule based solely on who calls and says, "Pastor, I've got to see you today."

Visioning

V indicates visioning for the future. If I have no future pictures, I'll live in the past. It's critical that you have a picture, because you become your life picture, as my book *UnLearning*

Church (Group Publishing, 2002) emphasizes. At Ginghamsburg Church one of our current pictures is to create a twenty-six-acre campus with forty-eight living units for at-risk children. It will be an interracial, intergenerational community of foster parents and senior adults who will receive reduced-rate housing for mentoring the children.

As the book of Jeremiah opens, the Lord asks the prophet twice, *"What do you see?"* (Jer. 1:11, 13). It's important to see and develop the picture God has given you. You can't live someone else's picture. You have a unique calling; you must become who God has created you to be.

One characteristic of risk-takers and innovators is that they have a clear faith-picture of life. Like Joshua, they need courage to step into their dream (see Josh. 1:1-9). Like Jeremiah, they must act upon everything God has commanded them, or they will yield to fear. I worry about twenty-something church leaders who have great potential, and yet begin to yield to the mean-spirited negativity of the godmothers and godfathers of the church. They begin to relinquish their dreams to fear, and then they downsize God's vision.

Eating and Exercise

E stands for eating and exercise. With the Apostle Paul, I want to say "do as I do" in all areas of my life (see 1 Cor. 11:1), including the way I take care of my heart and health. I run regularly, work out with weights, and watch my fats, carbs, and sugars. As a result I have more energy now at age fifty-three than I had at age thirty-three. I've come a long way since my late-2000 heart scare.

Our church is United Methodist and belongs to the West Ohio Conference, which represents almost 1,300 pastors. In 2004 we spent more money on health care for clergy than on mission. That is a painful reality. Our district superintendent sends out pedometers, asking each clergyperson to walk 10,000 steps a day. Our churches are filled with obese people who got that way simply through poor eating and inadequate exercise. That's both pulpit and pew. Obesity is a leading cause of preventable death in

America, with deaths attributed to this disease numbering hundreds of thousands a year.

Model for Living

The acronym D-R-I-V-E has become my way of life. Romans 12:1 says, "*To offer your bodies as a living sacrifice, holy and pleasing to God—this is true worship.*" These are the disciplines that help me grow, all of them contributing to my whole-life relationship with Jesus Christ. Faith + discipline is essential to creating momentum for life.

What's your model for living? What foundation are you laying

Faith + discipline is essential to creating momentum for life.

that will enable you to thrive when you hit resistance? Many church leaders don't have an action plan for a well-balanced life. If you don't have a self-leadership model that works for you, I challenge you to test and explore this one.

Momentum Busters

To go where God is calling in your life and vocation, you must deal with the momentum busters of rationalization ("I make myself the exception"), procrastination ("I don't know where to start"), and the lack of visualization ("I don't have a picture of where I am going").

Any of these attitudes can prevent you from moving toward the purpose for which God has created you.

Rationalization: "I Make Myself the Exception"

Jerusalem is nicknamed "the city set on a hill" for good reason. It is poetically called "*the city of our God...beautiful in elevation...the joy of all the earth*" (Ps. 48:1-2, NRSV).

My wife and I once stayed in Jerusalem in January. The temperature was hovering close to 30°F. The city is situated on an uneven rocky plateau at an elevation of some 2,500 feet.

Yet a half-hour later, only fourteen miles away at the Dead Sea, the lowest place on earth, the temperature was 40 degrees higher. The elevation from Jerusalem to the Dead Sea drops by 3,800 feet.

In ancient times, every faithful Jew (Israelite) was expected to make the pilgrimage to Jerusalem at least once a year. The place of worship at the top of the Temple mount is the place God had designated for people to make an honorable, excellent offering. The Temple was the only place to make this faithful offering to God. If you want to make an excellent offering to God, you can't stay on the plain; you must move up the hill!

No matter where you came from, to reach the Temple, the holy place of God, you faced quite a climb. It was not a morning stroll, but an intense journey that took mental preparation and rigorous physical effort. This journey involved the pilgrim's full commitment of body, mind, and spirit.

Worshipers, while making the ascent to The Holy City, sang what are called the Psalms of Ascent. These songs are about reinforcing character, faith, and persistence in the face of resistance. We find them in the Bible today as Psalms 120 to 134.

God teaches us through these psalms that faith is a journey of ascent. One of our dangers is to rationalize, telling ourselves that we can live at the top without the effort of the climb. "I make myself the exception," we tell ourselves.

I often run on a treadmill. I can do a speed of 7.4 for half an hour with an incline of 0 and have no problems. Sometimes I'll put the incline on 1 or 2; I feel the difference, but I can still make it through the run.

Faith is a journey of ascent. Our danger is to rationalize, telling ourselves that we can live at the top without the effort of the climb.

Once in a while at the gym someone who knows me will come by and press the "increase" button, moving the incline level up to 10. I feel it immediately as my heart rate increases and my body responds to the challenge.

God is like the person punching the incline button. God allows the resistance of incline to toughen me up. As God

God strengthens our life momentum by allowing resistance to come into our lives.

increases the incline of my path, my heart rate increases, which raises my passion, which fuels my momentum. We grow through resistance. We learn to strive and thrive through resistance. The radical nature of the incline equips us with the momentum we need to ascend the mountain. God strengthens our life momentum by allowing resistance to come into our lives.

I need momentum to move upward; everyone does. Nick Hoover, a twenty-seven-year-old from the Ginghamsburg Church community, participates in one of our three-times-a-week exercise classes. Nick says the feeling of being on a team has helped him deal with physical discipline as well as every other area of his life. He rises at 7:00 AM and makes it to the church gym for a 7:30 workout. "I feel like I'm on a team, training with accountability," he says. "I know if I miss, someone will ask me why I wasn't there." After two years, Nick has lost forty pounds and is a lot more energetic. He even ran his first official race. "Once you get going, it forms a habit," he says. "I feel better than I did in high school. I want to keep the momentum going. I don't want to regain the weight. I don't want to go back to the old Nick." He's not likely to go back if he keeps hanging out with others who have momentum.

I may be pleased with my physical condition but, like Nick, unless I work out I won't stay at my current level, much less gain ground. Followers of Jesus are

We're in a partnership with God that requires sweat equity on our part!

called to "work out" our salvation knowing *"it is God who works in you to will and to act in order to fulfill his good purpose"* (Phil. 2:12-13). We're in a partnership with God that requires sweat equity on our part!

From Genesis to Revelation, we are called to a lifestyle of holiness—*"without which no one will see the Lord"* (Heb. 12:14). Holiness is whole-life living. It means we are being transformed into God's likeness. It means our lives reflect the excellence of God.

All areas of our life must work together to reflect the excellence of God's character.

Eternal life equals *quality* of life, where each part of me reflects the excellence of Christ's character. Many people think of eternal life only as *quantity* of life—being saved forever. Salvation is eternal, but if we don't participate with Christ in the life-transformation of others, and ourselves, then we won't have the quality of life that matches the excellence of Christ.

Psalm 122 uses architecture to illustrate the excellence of Christ as the perfect order of God. Jerusalem is *"built like a city that is closely compacted together"* (v. 3). Everything fits: stone upon stone, and row upon row. The psalmist looks forward to being in a place that represents the ultimate integrated wholeness of God: *"I rejoiced with those who said to me, 'Let us go to the house of the* LORD*'"* (v. 1).

You don't just wake up one day and find yourself in a perfect world like the metaphor of Jerusalem's Temple, where everything represents the perfect order of God. You need a momentum that will carry you all the way up the hill of eternity. Our offering to God is a lifestyle that reflects God's excellence.

Why We Rationalize

We live in a culture that has a passion for the immediate. We want the "CliffsNotes" version of God: happiness, success, and fulfilling relationships. We want "easy" and "now," and we try to make God work that way too. This cult of the instant has created an aversion to sweat. Avoiding perspiration at all costs, we lower the bar. We change God's standard of measure. We turn to sex for sex's sake. "Why, God, did you create me with these urges?" we ask. Convincing ourselves that a loving God would never make life that hard, we lower the bar by having sex apart from the commitment to a lifelong, intimate relationship. Or we imagine ourselves having an affair with one of the desperate housewives on Wisteria Lane. I've heard that as many as one in four men struggle with addiction to Internet pornography—that's a lowered bar.[1]

Some have sold out by working for money rather than meaning, and settling for a job rather than God's purpose. We buy bigger cars and more toys for our personal pleasure, forgetting that Jesus said, "*the road is hard that leads to life*" (Matt. 7:13, NRSV). By lowering the bar, we arrogantly argue with what we read in the Bible, making ourselves the exception to God's created moral order. The call of Jesus is to journey on the narrow road. We downplay Jesus' warning that "*the gate is wide and the road is easy that leads to destruction, and there are many who take it*" (Matt. 7:13, NRSV). Yet we rationalize, "That doesn't really mean me." Trouble is, we're not just to believe Jesus but also to embrace the spirit and lifestyle of Jesus. The road is hard, and rationalizing in one area guarantees that you'll end up rationalizing in every area of life.

If you rationalize in one area, you'll end up rationalizing in every area of life.

Some people think their destination is to make a lot of money and retire in the Sunbelt, but that's a downsized goal! The destination of the Christ follower is not a retirement community of comfort but a continual journey of ascent where God's purpose comes first. We are to seek first the kingdom of God (Matt. 6:33). We want to be wherever the reign of God is present.

Some of us have momentum in one area of our lives, but plateau in others. You may be moving upward in your career but have grown stagnant in your marriage. I had momentum in ministry but lacked it in my relationship with my wife.

Some of us have momentum in one area of our lives, but plateau in others.

Some have it in both ministry and marriage but not in their physical bodies. A friend, Len Sweet, asked me ten years ago, "Mike, what's up with your weight?" I was rationalizing the typical American pound-and-a-half annual weight gain that had resulted in an out of shape forty-three-year-old. "Your weight doesn't reflect the excellence of God," he observed.

Too many Christians ignore and excuse our sin of gluttony (Prov. 23:21). Remember, all leadership begins with self-leadership. If I can't lead myself, I can't really lead anyone else, nor can you. Until your physical body experiences the momentum of ongoing care, you won't reach your full potential in influencing other people. A lowered bar of physical health affects the momentum of energy, spirit and influence. Our bodies are the housing for the eternal God, vessels to house the energy of God's powerful presence.

Proverbs 31 speaks of an excellent wife who is also a business entrepreneur and investor. Ever planning ahead, she teaches wisdom and kindness along the way. She's not driven by selfish achievement but by a virtue that reaches far beyond her family. *"She opens her arms to the poor, and extends her hands to the needy"* (v. 20). The main emphasis is on her character, but notice that *"she makes her arms strong"* (v. 17, NRSV) and *"she gets up while it is still night"* (v. 15). She has physical stamina and conditioning as well. She reflects momentum in every area of D-R-I-V-E: devotion to God, readiness for lifelong learning, investing in key relationships, visioning for the future, and eating and exercise for physical strength.

Time to Repent

The opening words of the first Psalm of Ascent, sung at the beginning of the journey, are prayers of repentance. As they began their journey, worshipers sang, "I cry to the Lord... 'Deliver me, O Lord, from lying lips, from a deceitful tongue'" (Ps. 120:1-2, NRSV). In other words, "Deliver me from my rationalization and compromise."

What have I been rationalizing about that isn't reflecting the excellence of God? I can name several areas. What about you? What rationalized sweat-avoiding habits can you name that you must deal with? Get busy "working out" your salvation.

Procrastination: "I Don't Know Where to Start"

Procrastination is huge momentum buster. Failure comes in direct proportion to procrastination.

Have you ever gone into a test unprepared? Procrastination, or the failure to take adequate measures of preparation, feeds feelings of inadequacy and creates self-doubt. You've probably had the dream about taking a critical exam for which you failed to study, a play for which you hadn't memorized the lines, or an important presentation where you were embarrassed to discover yourself standing alone in your underwear. Procrastination comes back to haunt you in your dreams. It attaches itself to your psyche and continues to raise its ugly head through feelings of anxiety and dreams marked by panic, failure, and defeat.

Here's how it happens to me. I graduated from college thirty years ago, yet I still have this occasional recurring nightmare. I'm in class, it's exam day, and all quarter long I've forgotten about the class. I didn't show up even once. "I'm not going to graduate," I tell myself in great anxiety. Then I wake up—and I'm actually sweating. In real life, I know this is absurd. I graduated from college. I also have a master's degree and a doctorate! Yet look what deep roots developed from the seeds of my old procrastination habits. They are so firmly rooted in my psyche that three decades later they can cause physical symptoms.

Procrastination is destructive, not just in what we put off today but in how it attaches itself to the subconscious mind and begins to reproduce itself. "As he thinketh in his heart, so is he," says Proverbs 23:7 (KJV). Our inner, subconscious thoughts determine who and what we become.

Procrastination Leads to Poverty

The instructor in Proverbs asks, "How long will you lie there, O lazybones? When will you rise from your sleep? A little sleep, a little slumber, a little folding of the hands to rest, and poverty will come upon you like a robber, and want, like an armed warrior" (6:9, NRSV).

Procrastination always makes you poor. It leads to poverty, not only in your wallet but also in your spirit as well.

During one season of my life I was experiencing success in ministry, yet my marriage was poverty-stricken because I was trying to run it on autopilot. There were things I knew I needed to do in my marriage, but I was procrastinating—putting them off until another day. Most people do well in one area of their lives, though they experience poverty in others.

Compromise in any one area of my life will eventually become an idolatrous cancer that will ultimately consume the rest.

Compromise in any one area of my life will eventually become an idolatrous cancer that will ultimately consume the rest. Procrastination, failing to do today what shouldn't be put off until tomorrow, sows seeds of lifetime failure.

Set Apart for God

God calls us to a lifestyle of holiness. "*Be holy*," the Bible commands at least two dozen times. The term *holiness* may sound impractical or otherworldly to the modern ear, but it actually means wholeness. When your life is set apart for God, your life is made whole or complete because it is devoted to the excellent purposes of God. Perhaps holiness should be spelled as (w)holiness. God is a God of whole-life excellence. Every dimension of God is excellent, yet in our brokenness we rationalize and procrastinate about areas in our lives that are less than excellent.

In one of the early Psalms of Ascent, the worshipers make a commitment to go to God's prescribed place of promise, and they pledge to do so with a positive, proactive attitude. "*I was glad when they said to me, 'Let us go to the house of the Lord'*" (Ps. 122:1, NRSV).

I won't be content with anything less than the excellent purpose of God, seeking God's prosperity in every area of my life. "*For the sake of the house of the LORD our God, I will seek your prosperity*" (Ps. 122:9). Every area of my life needs to become an honorable, excellent offering to God.

What happens when you put off until tomorrow what you know you need to do today? When you don't know how or where to start (or you *do* know and just plain don't want to do it!)? We find procrastination showing up in three different ways.

1. Defaulting. We make a commitment to do what's right and to tackle the true priority, but at the last minute we default and do something less urgent or more comfortable.

To write this book, for instance, I made the commitment to stay home and work in my office on Tuesdays. I had my coffee and devotion, ran on my treadmill for the day, showered, ate, and then dutifully opened my computer. "Okay, first paragraph, I'm ready for you to appear," I'd announce.

Actually, it wasn't smooth like that. Before opening my computer, I'd sweat just thinking about what was ahead. When I was finally sitting in front of my computer, I'd ask the appropriate question of my priority for that day: "What's a good opening for this chapter?" But after all of twelve seconds of looking at a blank screen, I'd shift, telling myself, "Hmmm. Nothing jumping out at me. Maybe I'll check my email." Somehow the less-urgent matter takes over all morning. Suddenly it's noon and I haven't written anything for the book yet, but I've devised yet another angle of procrastination: "Well, half the day is gone, so I'll just wait until next Tuesday to start again."

"But you don't know my schedule," you protest. "I'm not putting things off; life is just too crazy right now for me to cover everything that needs to be done."

Many ancient worshipers never made the pilgrimage to the house of God because they felt overwhelmed by the preparations and hassles. In the winter it snows in Jerusalem, and in the summer it's hot. "It's not such a good day to go up to the house of the Lord," people would procrastinate. In the between seasons, they might cite problems with not having the right clothes, too much traffic, feeling uncomfortable in crowds, and not knowing what to do with the kids. "It's easier to stay home," many people would conclude. But nothing worthwhile is easy, and the road to the house of God has always been narrow.

You've got to deal with your big "but"—the big procrastination statements you tell yourself. "But I don't have time to get close to God" or "but I don't have time to exercise because I'm too busy." What's *your* biggest "but"?

- D—If you're too busy to give time to talking to your Creator—that's what **devotion** actually is—then you're defaulting to lesser tasks.
- R—If the tyranny of the urgent squelches your **readiness** for lifelong learning, then you're defaulting to lesser tasks.
- I—If you don't have any room in your life to **invest** in key relationships, then you're defaulting to lesser tasks.
- V—If there is no room to **vision** toward the future, then you're defaulting to lesser tasks.
- E—If you don't have time to **exercise** or **eat** right, you're not recognizing your body as the temple of God. You're defaulting to less urgent tasks, or you're...

2. Overwhelmed. Some people feel they have so much to do that they don't know where to get started. The pile of ironing has stacked up for four weeks, and you have only two clean shirts left, and even they require deodorant in unlikely places. You don't know where to start, so you go to the refrigerator and dig into some Ben and Jerry's ice cream.

When you're feeling overwhelmed, you must do the first hard thing. In your house, it may mean to do fifteen minutes of ironing before you open the refrigerator again. In your spiritual house, it may mean to take a fifteen-minute walk around your block, putting all your cares onto God before you begin your task list. "*Cast all your anxiety on him because he cares for you*" (1 Pet. 5:7).

Good intentions or professions of belief are not the same thing as commitment. No matter how well intentioned, many folks don't make the commitment to finish the journey. In faith development, altitude requires a journey of exertion. Make the commitment to do the first thing.

That First Worst Step

My wife and I have a six-year-old giant schnauzer named Luka. He loves to be wherever we are. Whether we're cooking, watching TV, or working out, Luka likes to hang out with us.

He has a little problem, though. We call it the procrastination shuffle. Suppose we're upstairs and we call him to join us. He'll put one paw on the bottom step, and then he'll pause. "Nope!" his brain signals. Then he pulls that paw back, puts the other paw on the first step, leans forwards—and pauses again. Getting started is a real challenge for this 125-pound dog. We've watched him do his procrastination shuffle for as long as two minutes. (View Luka's procrastination shuffle at www.ginghamsburg.org/mfl.)

Finally he begins the climb. Once he gets started he's okay, but often he expends more energy to take that first step than to climb the entire staircase.

I'm like that too. When I get a feeling about something that I should be doing, how do I respond? Too often the biggest temptation is to take two aspirin and go to bed until the feeling goes away.

I'm not alone. There's even an official term for a speaker's or author's procrastination dilemma: writer's block. Anne Lamott, one of my top-shelf authors, talks about getting herself started by writing "shitty" first drafts.[2] You have to make the commitment to start somewhere.

You have to make the commitment to start somewhere.

"Almost all good writing begins with terrible first efforts," says Anne Lamott in *Bird by Bird* (Pantheon, 1994).[3] The title's metaphor came from her brother, who at ten years old was trying to write a report on birds. He'd had three months to write, and it was due the next day. "He was at the kitchen table close to tears, surrounded by binder paper and pencils, and unopened books on birds, immobilized by the hugeness of the task ahead. Then my father [an accomplished writer] sat down beside him, put his arm around my brother's shoulder, and said, 'Bird by bird, buddy. Just take it bird by bird.'"[4]

Suppose I keep reading about the need to eat better, but I'm confused. Everyone is talking about exercise and eating, but I'm overwhelmed and don't know where or how to begin.

I tried to start a fitness program on my own. I did five jumping jacks and started to sweat, so I figured I had gotten my heart going adequately for that day. I tried a few pushups. Going down was okay, but I had a lot of trouble pushing back up. Running was extremely uncomfortable. Actually, it seemed impossible. Too many parts of me bounced as I ran!

Not knowing where to start or change, I had zero momentum. I felt overwhelmed, and so I quit. I tried it another day, another week, and another month—and I quit each time long before I had any momentum to show for my good intentions. I couldn't lead myself past where I was. Nor can you.

My breakthrough was when I decided that I needed someone ahead of me, someone experiencing success that could get me unstuck. I needed a coach. I asked for a trainer.

I found Chastity Slone, a certified personal trainer from our Ginghamsburg Church family. She asked how well I could run, and she tested me with a moderate run around our church campus. After running for what felt like ten minutes, I began to complain, "We've got to stop and walk," I moaned. Unfortunately, I had gone only one minute, twenty-eight seconds according to Chastity's stopwatch! She wouldn't let me stop, saying, "If you stop it's almost impossible to get going again." This is the essence of momentum. Stop and it's almost impossible to get going again.

The essence of momentum: If you stop, it's almost impossible to get going again.

For lasting momentum, you need the accountability of a person who is ahead of you, someone who has demonstrated success, accomplishment, and faithfulness in the area in which you are struggling. This is where the church plays a powerful role. Our church is using a life-coach model, providing classes in everything from fitness to finances. If you commit to do the first hard thing, we'll commit to help you get there. We want your whole life—body, soul, and spirit—to become an honorable, excellent offering to God.

Many people at Ginghamsburg Church are doing a *Transformation Journal*,[5] a daily Scripture journal designed to take us deeper in devotion to God. Every Wednesday night, we have a life coach, Pastor Mike Bowie, teach on the *Journal* Scriptures, taking people to the next level of growth. We offer classes in a wide variety of areas where people typically get stuck. We all need coaches who are ahead of us.

3. Disorganization. Sometimes we procrastinate because we can't see our way through the clutter. When you allow cluttered spaces anywhere in your life, they lead to cluttered thinking, which translates to cluttered spirits and undisciplined lifestyles. God is a God of order!

The metaphor used in Ps. 122:3 is of the dwelling of God that is well-designed and strategically built. Jerusalem is *"built like a city that is closely compacted together."*

Architects begin by designing blueprints—a life map. Strategic lives likewise develop out of a well-designed blueprint. They work out of a disciplined plan.

You need a life map: a critical plan with definite starting point. If you allow a space to become undisciplined or disorganized, it grows and begins to take on a life of its own.

In recent years Carolyn's mom moved into a retirement center. Carolyn spent a week sorting through her mother's possessions. It was hard for her to give or throw away any of it; so many items had a specific meaning or special memory. Where could she put all the stuff? Our garage was the solution.

We built our own house in 1993, and we've always worked hard to keep our garage clean. Our two cars always fit nicely into the garage. But with the loads of furniture, boxes, and knick-knacks, our garage was full!

Then our son Jonathan came home from college. Our standard house rule had always been for anyone coming home from an extended time away to carry everything inside to his or her room, or to the storage room in the basement. But this time Jonathan didn't do all that. He didn't even ask to change the plan. He now saw the garage as a place of disorganization, and simply added all his college stuff to our growing monster in the garage.

Is your home or apartment like that? When you allow space for clutter, the pile somehow grows. This same idea works in the rest of your life. If you allow clutter in your spiritual life, marriage, finances, or anywhere else, it will grow. More clutter will accu-

mulate along the way. Soon you'll have a monster in your life. One holiday weekend, I told Jonathan to clean out his stuff. As an avid baseball player, he owned fifty broken bats. Each bat had a meaning, just like all the items in Carolyn's pile. For us, the roadmap was a boxful of garbage bags begging to be filled. The primary path we selected went from the garage to a garbage pile on the curb. The plan worked. I can now put two vehicles (and one motorcycle!) back into our garage.

If you allow clutter in your spiritual life, marriage, finances, or anywhere else, it will grow.

What's your life map to holiness—to wholeness? Where are you making a less-than-honorable offering to God?

Poor Visualization:
"I Don't Have a Picture of Where I Am Going"

The Bible says, "*where there is no vision, the people perish*" (Prov. 29:18, KJV). To have vision is to have the ability to see with eyes of faith. Vision knows how to articulate God's promising possibilities for the future. The Psalms of Ascent are a constant reminder to see, from God's perspective, both the world and our own purpose in it. As the ascent becomes steeper, we need a clear reminder of why we started the climb in the first place.

With the ancient pilgrims, we call on God because we need help: "*I call on the LORD in my distress, and he answers me*" (Ps. 120:1). We want to see life from

As the ascent becomes steeper, we need a clear reminder of why we started the climb in the first place.

the perspective of heaven: "*I lift up my eyes to you, to you who sit enthroned in heaven*" (Ps. 123:1). As dangers and temptations lurk around the perilous bend, we need to hang on to the vivid picture of our destination.

The pilgrims who were on ascent visualized standing inside the gates of Jerusalem long before they ever arrived: "*Our feet are* standing in your gates, Jerusalem" (Ps. 122:2). Vision creates momentum that is self-sustaining and self-fulfilling.

One of the five life practices for balance and self-leadership in D-R-I-V-E is the practice of visualization. An entire future chapter ("Visioning for the Future") will focus on seeing ahead through eyes of faith.

The momentum of God's purpose and dream is too great for any of us not to reflect the excellent character of God in any one area of our lives. The Christian has made a commitment to a lifetime journey of faith. Following Jesus is hard. We are to go where Jesus is going, to be who Jesus is being, and to do what Jesus is doing. The Bible says to work out your salvation—that means a commitment to sweat! The great evangelist Dwight L. Moody said, "We pray like it is all up to God. We work like it is all up to us." Grace is not passive. Grace is active: Our sweat meets Jesus' blood, and that's where the miracle takes place.

Only you can make the commitment to start the climb.

The Apostle Paul says, *"... straining toward what is ahead, I press on toward the goal to win the prize for which God has called me heavenward in Christ Jesus"* (Phil. 3:13-14, NIV).

Today is the day of salvation. Today is the day your sweat needs to meet Jesus' blood.

Opportunity is not going to come along and drag you off the couch. You have to put yourself out there. Only you can make the commitment to start the climb.

What hard thing will you tackle first? Deal with your big "but" and take action today!

"Now is the time of God's favor, now is the day of salvation" (2 Cor. 6:2). Enter into God's fullness and wholeness.

Sustaining Momentum

This book is a five-week journey of ascent. Each of the following chapters introduces a daily life discipline around the acronym of D-R-I-V-E. These five life practices will enable you to build and sustain momentum to make your life an honorable, excellent offering and to reach God's promised destination.

Devotion: Begin each day with the practice of Bible study, meditation, journaling, and prayer.

Readiness for lifelong learning: Live like a child in school, no matter what your chronological age. Take some time each day for the purpose of growing in "life science." Become a student of the culture, so you can continue to make a meaningful contribution in God's world.

Investing in key relationships: Many leaders have fallen here. This is the everyday practice of keeping your heart first in the home and then investing in those people who are most strategic to the mission that God has called you to.

Visioning for the future: Look forward through eyes of faith. Articulate with clarity God's preferred future; make daily strategic corrections to your life picture.

Eating and exercise: Take small steps and then bigger ones, exercising your "push back" muscle at the next meal. Push yourself back from the table to go take a vigorous walk. Take care of your body for the long haul as well as find more energy for today.

These five activities are designed to reach God's purpose in your life and mine.

Before You Begin the Next Chapter

In what area are you not doing so well? Where are you stuck? Pause to name the specific momentum buster that you want to break through. It may be a favorite rationalization, a habit of procrastination, or an unhealthy picture of where your future is headed. Write a prayer of repentance, naming the specific area you want to work on in God's grace, making a commitment to cooperate with God in breaking this barrier.

Direct your prayer around Psalm 120:2.

> Deliver me, O Lord, from lying lips and a deceitful tongue. Save me from rationalization, procrastination, and a lack of visualizing your bigger purpose for my life mission. By faith I enter into your salvation from _____ [name of specific sin]. By faith I will work out my salvation by _____ [make commitment to a new discipline outlined in this book]. I welcome and invite the Holy Spirit's work in my life because of what Jesus did on the cross for me. Amen.

As you begin this climb, this journey of ascent, who can go with you? Who can hold you up in prayer? How can you help support someone else? Why not read this book with an accountability partner or in a group? You could cover the next five chapters as a five-week journey of discipline. Each chapter will offer a series of short questions, such as the ones listed on the following pages. Your group can help hold you accountable by talking about what you learn as you go through each chapter.

Momentum for Life Devotional — Individual

Read aloud the main Scripture, Psalm 122.

1. Jesus calls us, saying, "Follow me." Have you been an active follower or a passive believer?

2. Are you able to "sing through resistance" or do life's challenges overwhelm you? What is something you can *do* as an act of faith in order to keep moving forward when facing resistance?

3. Procrastination is a huge momentum-buster, but as our Master Designer, God is intent on ordering our lives as God did the city of Jerusalem (Ps. 122:3). What part of your life needs to be organized for God's glory? Where do *you* need to take charge?

4. A life-map can help us keep a future picture. Consider drawing a map of your own life and where you hear/see God leading you. What is up ahead on your map?

Momentum for Life Devotional — In a Group

Read aloud the main Scripture, Psalm 122.

1. "Conversions." Can you name the time and place of your last conversion? Share with the group.

2. Think of a place in your life that does not fully reflect the excellence of God. Share it out loud if you can.

3. What is a healthy step you would love to take or need to take, but can't yet imagine taking?

4. Are you rationalizing (making excuses) or procrastinating (don't know how to start) instead of taking your next step on the journey of ascent?

5. If you can, name your next conversion. Pray for one another and commit to being accountable to your group as you take charge of procrastination.

CHAPTER TWO

Devotion to God

DEVOTION> *Focused commitment of time and energy;
dedicated; faithful; deep affection.*

PASSIONATE> *Having or showing strong emotions.
Being intense, ardent, or rousing.*

*"Very early in the morning, while it was still dark,
Jesus got up, left the house and went off to a solitary
place, where he prayed." (Mark 1:35)*

Devotion and passion are twin emotions from the heart, powerful motivators that create the energy of momentum in our lives.
Many anointed leaders of God have discovered that emotional
passion is a greater persuasive force than cognitive belief in deter-
mining life direction and behavior.

King David was one such anointed leader. He had experienced
the hand of God working through his life in powerful ways,
becoming the greatest king Israel ever knew. He had been called
by God for a powerful purpose—to lead a unified nation that
honored and served God, one that ushered in an era of justice,
prosperity, and peace. He was known as a man of great faith and
confident passion. *"In your strength I can crush an army; with my
God I can scale any wall"* (2 Sam. 22:30, NLT).

David was a man after God's heart (I Sam. 13:14, Acts 13:22) and passionate about everything he did, from battling Goliath the God-mocker to planning the Grand Temple of God. David's passionate heart was vulnerable to less honorable endeavors, however. Following his own pleasures, he became obsessed with another man's wife, then passionately covered up this misguided mission. In a time of moral catastrophe, David's failure was not a result of his cognitive belief but of his unbridled passion.

In a similar way, Satan's attack through temptation against Jesus in the wilderness was not directed toward Jesus' beliefs but towards his human passions. *"After fasting forty days and forty nights, [Jesus] was hungry. The tempter came to him and said, 'If you are the Son of God, tell these stones to become bread'"* (Matt. 4:2-3). Satan tempted Jesus to shift the focus of his devotion away from his Father to food and fame. Evil went directly for the jugular vein of Jesus' human passions rather than simply trying to appeal to his cognitive beliefs.

The Smell of Passion

Devotion is what you care about, the focus of your deepest desires. People can sense your devotion. People can *smell* your passions. Belief, by contrast, is something you must verbally describe. I need to inform people of my beliefs.

My leadership at Ginghamsburg Church has been on an upward ascent for more than a quarter of a century, yet no one knows my political beliefs. I have never shared my political persuasions in a message, or allowed political issues to be the focus of my ministry.

One weekend I asked my congregation to tell me what I am passionate about. I was expecting them to respond, "Jesus!" but instead they shouted back in one voice, "BASEBALL!" Our church doesn't know my political views, but they can smell my passion.

I am indeed a baseball enthusiast, yet until that moment I didn't know it was that noticeable. I thought about how they responded. If baseball comes across as a greater passion in my life than God, then I need to realign my heart.

The same principle works at home. Our children pick up on our passion, far more than they hear our words. Our children are more influenced in their worldviews and life values by the object of our devotion than by our stated beliefs. Is it any wonder that they readily adopt our passions for music, money, movies, and athletics while struggling with our beliefs and tuning out our religious traditions after they leave home?

Devotion is about ultimate values. Devotion reveals true belief. Your greatest enthusiasm betrays your true object of worship. Whatever you worship drives you.

Whatever you worship drives you.

Motivation is boiled down to passion. Your passions, more than your beliefs, determine your life actions and directions.

Anyone who struggles with discipline issues or addictive behaviors understands the power of passion. Have you ever gone to a restaurant having made the decision ahead of time to pass on dessert, only to be derailed when the server showed you the dessert tray with triple-chocolate cheesecake? Your beliefs tell you that you don't need the high-cholesterol fat calories, but your appetite induces the drive. The servers are trained to know that your passions will prove stronger than your beliefs.

Most people think, "If only I could increase my belief in God, things would be different." Most likely it is not your *belief* in God that needs to increase; it is your *passion* for God that must increase in order to give you the momentum to thrive in resistance. Ask those who know you closely what your passions are, and they will tell you immediately.

Devotion is stronger than structures of intellectual belief. Devotion is what you ultimately care about, what you value. Whatever you ultimately value becomes the object of your worship, and what you worship *drives* you! We don't need to increase our belief in God—we need to increase our passion for God!

Present to God's Presence

I have found that it takes me about twenty-four hours to lose a healthy fear of God. When that happens, the devotions of my heart turn to counterfeit gods and lifeless sources. This is why I must begin each day with the lifelong discipline of devotion.

When I come home from work at the end of the day, I enter the house through the garage and into the laundry room. In passing through, I come to an eat-in kitchen that Carolyn and I both enjoy. It has a desk where we put the mail for each other to see. I find it relaxing to thumb through the mail when I first come home.

One evening, Carolyn was excited to tell me something, but my first impulse was to check the mail. Carolyn was chatting away about her day, but I was distracted. Partway through the discussion she said, "Wait a minute! I'm talking and you're not here!"

In the same way, God is always speaking, but we're not always present to the relationship. Does it ever seem to you like God is hiding? The real problem is that *we* are the ones who are not aware of God's presence.

Devotion is a focused time of being fully present to God's presence.

Devotion is a focused time of being fully present to God's presence. This becomes both hard work and intentional discipline. My God-stalking efforts involve Bible study, meditation on what I'm reading, prayer, and journaling—using our church's *Transformation Journal*. Later I will fully explain the **S.O.N.** method of daily devotion, which involves <u>S</u>cripture reading, <u>O</u>bservation and <u>N</u>aming the personal principle of the reflection that relates to my life in the present. These practices create in me an awareness of the presence of God, allowing the personal voice of God to speak to me and my life situation each day.

A More Passionate Life Focus

The daily practice of being fully present to God's presence renews a healthy, passionate life-focus. Psalm 121 is the second Psalm of Ascent. It begins, "*I lift up my eyes to the mountains— where does my help come from?*"

The phrase "*my help*" refers to my meaning, my purpose, and my life-empowerment. Metaphorically speaking, this journey of ascent is to the House of God, the place of God's ultimate purpose and presence in my life.

Many of us read these verses and recall a vision of nature in its pristine beauty. A hillside or mountainous setting, rich in color and awe, is a place of inspiration for many. Indeed, I love Pennsylvania's mountains. Each time I drive through them, they get me in touch with creation, and I think of God.

For the Israelite pilgrims who sang this psalm on the way up to Jerusalem's house of worship, however, the mountains held a different meaning. In the Jewish culture during the time when these psalms were written, the hills contained shrines and altars to pagan gods, counterfeits of the real thing. These subtle sirens tempted tourists to stop short of the ultimate objective. They presented the allure to come over and hang out, dabbling in their destructive influences.

You might compare these ancient pagan enterprises as counterparts to Alka Seltzer's promise of "plop, plop, fizz, fizz, oh, what a relief it is" for any ache or pain. The great temptation for any child of God is to stop short of true transformation and merely seek relief. Travelers could seek relief from many brands of over-the-counter gods that offered instant remedy for every traveling need. Worried about the stock market? The gods of fertility would guarantee the success of your produce. Fatigued by the heat? You could go to the sun priest and pray for protection from the elements. Suffering from emotional distress? The moon goddess could remove emotional pain for a small fee. Love-starved or driven by lust?

Sacred prostitutes, male and female, were available to relieve your sexual tension. The red-light district and porno chat rooms of today are nothing new.

I have been on a God-journey for thirty-some years. Life has at times become tiring and often feels difficult. Where do I find relief? The temptation is to look to the hills around me for some kind of immediate gratification. It would be easy enough to simply turn off the road on my way up the path to Jerusalem and the House of God. The temptation of the hills is to look for instant relief and gratification.

Many of these same influences are accepted in our culture as well, with incessant advertisements for over-the-counter gods, fast-food substitutes, and feel-good potions designed to help us avoid the strenuous climb of life. Many leaders have turned aside to the sound of the lustful siren on the path of ascent. One leader from a conservative denomination that I was consulting with told me that approximately one-third of the pastors in his district who were disciplined or removed from ministry lost their position because of sexual immorality or addiction to Internet pornography.

There are many gods of immediacy along the journey that make false claims by offering "Cliffs-Notes" versions of fulfillment, happiness, and meaning. You can purchase spells that will protect you from ills and spills, or provide the thrills for the perils of the road. As you ascend higher on the road of God's calling, the voices from the hills only grow louder in their attempt to lure you to the cultural shrines that make promises of immediate relief and self-gratification.

As you ascend higher on the road of God's calling, the voices grow louder in their attempt to lure you to promises of self-gratification.

Danger Zone

During this last half of my life, I am setting aside a few days several times a year to meet with small groups of pastors in a living room or retreat environment. It's one thing to mentor from a platform, speaking to conferences with hundreds or thousands in attendance. What I really want to do at this stage of my life is sit down on a couch and challenge young pastors face-to-face not to compromise in their own Song of Ascent.

Not long ago I met with two dozen young leaders, challenging them to be everything God created them to be. We held our pastor's practicum in Ginghamsburg's original 1876 church building on our south campus. Sitting in a comfortable chair, propping up my feet on an end table, I reminded them that all leadership begins with self-leadership. "You can't lead anyone farther than you're leading yourself," I explained. I told them about my acronym of D.R.I.V.E. "Before you can ever lead anybody else you have to be able to lead yourself, and it begins right here in these five daily disciplines."

One pastor had apparently been eyeing my boots as he listened to me share. At the first break of the morning he approached me and said, "Do you just wear those boots or do you really have a bike?" He had recognized my footwear as Harley-Davidson boots.

"I'm getting a bike next month," I answered with a big smile. It would be my first Harley. I'd spent sixteen years saving for it because of our family commitment to live debt-free as well as not to divert money earmarked for mission. God had used my delayed gratification to build character, but I was eager for my bike's delivery date and had already purchased my riding boots. On that day I had them on, breaking them in.

This young pastor asked a great question. He knew the power of the boots and the lure of the bike; he was the proud owner of a Harley!

The danger is that our passions tend to take on a life of their own. The hillside shrines call to me as I move into the section of the path marked "mid-life crisis." I have been on this journey for a long time, and where does my relief come from? Potential passions beckon from the hills. "Come over here and we will give you life," they claim.

I shouldn't be surprised when my eyes are pulled from the road of ascent to the distraction of the hillside shrines. Passions promise us—they tempt us saying, "Hey, it's not hard! Come over here and I will give you life!" Harley-Davidson has worked hard to create a cult-like culture with its life-offering promises. The company's slogan is "Live to Ride, Ride to Live" and I find myself anxious to buy the leathers, ride, and find my life's passion.

Danger zone! *"Do not turn to idols or make metal gods for yourselves,"* Leviticus 19:4 states, *"I am the LORD your God."* Along with many others, I can be easily tempted towards idolatry, showing greater passion for metal than for God. It takes me about twenty-four hours to lose my focus on God. That's why the first discipline of each morning involves an intense practice of being fully present to God's presence. I am then reminded, *"Surely the [idolatrous] commotion on the hills and mountains is a deception; surely in the LORD our God is the salvation of Israel"* (Jer. 3:23). I remember that my help is not found in the promised relief of the hills but that *"my help comes from the LORD, the Maker of heaven and earth"* (Ps. 121:2).

> **It takes me about twenty-four hours to lose my focus on God.**

Wrestling Match

I am drawn to the story of Jacob in Genesis 32. Jacob was going through some kind of peril on life's journey. He was literally in the midst of a process of ascent, and all night long he wrestled with God, who had come to him in some kind of physical form. God said to Jacob, *"Let me go!"* and Jacob replied, *"I am not going to let you go until you bless me."*

This does not translate into slipping into church on Sunday, then going back home and automatically enjoying the blessing of God. God doesn't respond to the "really quick, bottom line, right now, here I am" method of devotion. It's all about the relationship. I have been in this relationship with God thirty-plus years, and intimacy in any relationship is hard work. It's an everyday kind of discipline, and I must be willing to hang on to God, to work until resolution and connection emerge. If I let go of God too soon, I am done!

As with Jacob, the residual limp reminds me of my daily dependence. Anyone who has wrestled in school knows that wrestling is a hot, sweaty, uncomfortable discipline. Miracles are not magic. Anything worthwhile in life comes from a sustained momentum in the same direction.[6] There is nothing quick about a leaving a legacy. There's nothing easy about mining the true meaning out of our existence.

Anything worthwhile in life comes from a sustained momentum in the same direction.

Jacob discovered that the God of his ancestors is not to be manipulated for selfish purposes or instant relief and gratification. Simple Sunday school solutions will not suffice in the ascent through the postmodern fog of the world as we know it. These quick remedies offer spiritual meaning while denying absolute truth. Jacob grabbed hold of God and refused to let go. "I will not...I cannot...I must not let go until I live in your (w)holiness!"

In Oprah Winfrey's O magazine, I read about a woman trying to find answers for life in Buddhism. She begins, "The God of my childhood is not what I am after. What I am seeking is a rugged, everyday type of deity—one that can provide a compassionate lens through which to view my life, a split-second of serenity between the moment the milk gets spilled on my new cashmere sweater and my reaction. I need a spiritual practice, if only to comfort myself that while I am clearly getting older, I'm doing my level best to get wiser, too."[7]

God-wrestling is an everyday practice. Any wrestler or athlete understands the discipline and energy required to be fit for a match. Likewise, every day I need to challenge my worldview against the worldview of Jesus. I am constantly tempted to use Jesus' name but to live out of the soft-secular worldview that is so predominant in the culture of our churches.

Many people in the Church do the same thing. They name Jesus' name but still trust materialism to provide meaning and security.

When you make a donation, you don't alter your lifestyle; it doesn't cost you anything.

This is why most of us merely donate to God. When you make a donation, you don't alter your lifestyle; it doesn't cost you anything.

Jesus calls us to sacrifice, to go the way of the cross. Sacrifice is when you willfully alter your lifestyle for a higher, greater purpose. Every day I must wrestle with God to remind me of the why and the Who of my life. This practice of devotion, my 6:00 AM wrestling match, renews my life focus; if I let go of God too soon, I am done.

The Jesus Movement

One of most incredible changes I've seen in my years of ministry has been the marginalization of Christian influence in Western civilization.

Some may remember the Jesus movement of the 1970s. I was part of it. Growing up, I related much more to rock music than to the liturgical Christian year of my childhood. Then in the 1970s Campus Crusade for Christ at the University of Cincinnati had a powerful impact on my life. Our meetings were often the raw, living room atmosphere of a counter-cultural movement.

I wasn't alone in my newfound faith. It seemed everyone was talking about Jesus, from athletes like former Dallas Cowboy star Roger Stauback, to presidents like Jimmy Carter, and even to several beauty queens who won the Miss America pageant. A number of other prominent people looked into Christianity, such as musician Bob Dylan in his album "Slow Train Coming." Even the *Tonight Show* band leader Doc Severinsen was converted for a season!

With so much conversation about Jesus, most of us thought we were on the verge of a global spiritual awakening. We naively thought that if Jesus had radically changed our lives, we could connect Jesus into others' cultural contexts and their lives could be radically changed as well. While this era had all the earmarks of a Jesus revolution, we compromised the true values of the kingdom of God. We traded the revolution for the relevance of secular culture.

Consequently, the Church of the twenty-first century struggles with spiritual impotency. Researcher George Barna reminds us that 95 percent of the people in church never bring another person to church with them.[8] More powerfully, he finds that while 120 million attend church on a regular basis, only fifteen million—less than 10 percent—grasp the message that significance in life is not dependent on our income or personal success.[9]

A Jesus Worldview

I must continually challenge my worldview against the worldview of Jesus. A worldview is a set of fundamental beliefs that determine your primary life values, decisions, and actions. Your worldview has more to do with your values than your religion. Your worldview sets the course of your life action. A worldview determines everything from your sexual mores to your political persuasions.

Your worldview has more to do with your values than your religion.

Tim Keller, who is lead pastor at Redeemer Presbyterian Church in New York City (www.redeemer.com), has good insight on the types of worldviews found in North American churches today. Redeemer's vision is to renew New York City socially, spiritually, and culturally. Tim talks about the diversity of worldviews in American culture. I am synthesizing these into four predominant worldviews found in the institutional church today.

1. Secular. People with a secular worldview are skeptical of anything supernatural. They may or may not believe in some sort of higher power, but they live their lives within the confines of human logic. They make clear distinctions between secular and sacred. They believe that to involve faith in the daily marketplace of life is tantamount to superstition. They see belief in a supernatural God as a barrier to social progress. Theirs is a humanistic point of view, with the basic premise that human beings have a universal need to create their own meaning, values and destiny.

They view the world solely in materialistic terms, convinced that nothing exists outside of matter—the molecules that make up people and things. People and things are the only resources available to solve all the problems of life.

Human beings have a universal need to create their own meaning, values, and destiny.

You'll find relatively few people with this mindset as regular church attenders. Most secular people in North America are Caucasian, over the age of forty, and from Protestant-Catholic-Jewish backgrounds. They control most of the elite academic institutions in this country. They also run the universities in North America that were formerly run by churches, ranging from Harvard (originally started to train ministers) to most universities formerly connected with a specific denomination. For example, more than one hundred colleges and universities are United Methodist affiliated. Most were "designed for evangelism" but have been "swept up…into the culture and purposes of the American academy,"[10] according to *The Dying of the Light: The Disengagement of Colleges and Universities from Their Christian Churches*. It cites as representative the university chaplain, a United Methodist cleric, who describes his responsibility, as he sees it, to "defend the importance of the university as a secular culture against all forms of orthodoxy."[11]

2. Soft-secular. The worldview most predominant in churches is "soft-secular." People with a soft-secular worldview believe in God and claim a faith identity—Jewish, Protestant, or Catholic—yet God is a secondary value or belief. They may confess Jesus but trust the values of secular culture, putting their trust in material possessions to provide meaning rather than trusting God's promise of provision. They make religious donations rather than life sacrifices. It is difficult for soft-secular people to make significant time or financial commitments to their churches.

Even though they believe in God, God is not their first priority or passion. They live comfortably in two spheres, sacred and secular, but when pressed for time their default always goes to the secular. They bring Jesus into their worldview instead of being converted into his.

People with a soft-secular mindset represent the predominant worldview in baby-boomer churches.

People with a soft-secular mindset tend to be over the age of forty. They represent the predominant worldview in baby-boomer churches.

3. Post-secular. A third worldview is more widespread in people under the age of forty. It's found in what some call millennial churches or Gen X churches. It's the post-secular view, more commonly referred to as "postmodern." Post-secular people are open to the supernatural but biased toward an expressive individualism. "It's true if it works for me," they believe. Those who view life this way are centered in today. The present is all that matters, and anything in the past is irrelevant to the expression of self and truth. Likewise, commitments made today—such as the "I do" of marriage—are viewed as intentions that may or may not work for tomorrow or the future.

For post-secular people, when maintaining identification with Jesus means a missed opportunity for a sexual encounter or a professional advancement, they bail on their Christian commitment.

Many times I see post-secular people make what seems to be a heartfelt commitment to Jesus, but when identification with Jesus means a missed opportunity for a relationship, a sexual encounter, or a professional advancement, they bail on the Christian commitment. Post-seculars attempt to fit Christ into their own worldview instead of being transformed into his, creating a cult of self. Sadly, this is the worldview of many in the Church.

Taking on the Worldview of Jesus

The Christian worldview says that commitment to Christ is bigger than my life or my lifetime. Truth will work and prevail because it is true, but it may not prevail in my lifetime. In fact, living for truth may cost me my life. Ouch!

Jesus said, *"For whoever wants to save their life will lose it, but whoever loses their life for me will save it"* (Luke 9:24). His call, to deny ourselves and take up Jesus' cross daily (Luke 9:23) for the sake of the coming kingdom of God, is the only way we can find life. This worldview flies in the face of the soft-secular mindset found so widely in churches. Life is not about me right now but about me being a link in the chain of God's generations. It's not about my wants, my passions, or my needs, but it is about my commitment to God's greater purpose and the coming of the kingdom of God! The sacred trust I have from all generations is to connect the covenant of the past with the promised coming kingdom, knowing from Jesus' warning that pain may be part of the package. Obeying the truth may lead to ostracism, loss of relationship, persecution, and rejection in my lifetime.

Obeying the truth of God may lead to smaller churches, like the small group of followers who hung with Jesus. After all, his church consisted of only 120 people at the time of his death. Many of us would not consider this an indicator of ministry success. He would not have been asked to speak at a conference on the subject of breaking the 200 barrier. Perhaps we are working from a faulty measure of success, driven by the values of our culture and not the kingdom of God.

We need to rethink church and to reimagine it from God's perspective. For a moment, imagine that the secular parts of our culture have no sway over you. Forget also what your bishop, church board, or church polity book require of you. From Micah 6:8 take a reality check: *"What does the LORD require of you? To act justly and to love mercy and to walk humbly with your God."* Notice the verb in this passage: to *act*, not to *believe*. Likewise, the account of the early church is called the *Acts* of the Apostles, not the *beliefs* of the apostles. Not even the *intentions* of the apostles!

Isaiah 58 talks about a faith group who embodied a soft-secular view of spiritual renewal. They had been fasting, gathering for instruction, and praying—all the right things for all the wrong reasons. They did all the religious rituals, with none of the spiritual power. "Where are you, God?" they ask. God tells them, in essence, "I'm not interested in how many butts you put in chairs at your weekend services." Power with God is a result of our actions toward people. *"Is not this the kind of fasting I have chosen: to loose the chains of injustice and untie the cords of the yoke, to set the oppressed free and break every yoke? Is it not to share your food with the hungry and to provide the poor wanderer with shelter?"* (v. 6-7).

This is not just an Old Testament issue. Jesus reiterated: *"Whatever you did for one of the least of these brothers and sisters of mine, you did for me"* (Matt. 25:40). To have Jesus' worldview is to reach out to those on the fringes; those who don't fit into the institutional church. *"For I was hungry and you gave me something to eat, I was thirsty and you gave me something to drink, I was a stranger and you invited me in, I needed clothes and you clothed me, I was sick and you looked after me, I was in prison and you came to visit me"* (Matt. 25:35-36).

Jesus had a passionate mission: *"to seek and save what was lost"* (Luke 19:10). Not those who were already safe on the inside but those who had no idea how to get in. His mission was to reach the lost sheep of Israel, Jewish people who did not relate to or feel welcomed into traditional Temple worship. Even more specifically, he focused on a certain economic group—those on margins of the economic culture: the poor, the prisoners, the blind, and the oppressed (Luke 4:18). At Ginghamsburg, we've translated Jesus' mission to focus on people who are tuned out or turned off by traditional Church.

Donation vs. Sacrifice

The majority of people in our churches do not have a Christian worldview.

The majority of people in our churches do not have a Christian worldview. They believe in Jesus and profess Jesus, but they still draw their meaning and security from the materialistic values of secular culture. Most churchgoers are soft-secular people who have stopped short of being converted to a truly Christian worldview. Many people who say they believe the Bible literally, even fundamentalists, are not converted to its worldview. It's easy to profess faith and make a donation, but quite another to take up the cross and make a living sacrifice.

What about you? Do you measure success by the size of your organization? Have you sacrificed the revolution implicit in the kingdom of God in the name of cultural relevance?

Size is not the measure of strength. It's not how fat you are but how fit you are. Jesus must have understood this because he led a powerful movement of 120 people at the end of his earthly ministry. I'd much rather share ministry with 120 revolutionaries than lead thousands coming merely to hear how to live a bit better in their lives. Attendance is not the measure of faithfulness. Sacrifice is the measure of faithfulness, offering our bodies as living sacrifices (Rom. 12:1-2). *"Whatever you did for one of the least of these,"* Jesus reminds us, *"You did for me"* (Matt 25:40). Worship must challenge a person's worldview against the worldview of Christ Jesus. All the bells and whistles in our postmodern worship experiences cannot give us life if the gospel is lost. Fitness, not fatness, will determine the depth of our spiritual lives and our organization's effectiveness.

The distractions on the hillside tempt us to stop short of Jesus' call to journey the way of the cross. *"Whoever wants to be my disciple must deny themselves and take up their cross daily and follow me"* (Luke 9:23). It is hard work to persevere through pain and the rigorous daily discipline of self-denial. The temptation is to stop short of the city of God and to set up camp at the seductive altar of the "have-it-your-way" idols. Many people in the Church believe in God but draw their comfort, meaning, and security from secular culture.

Many people in the church believe in God but draw their comfort, meaning, and security from secular culture.

Beginning my day in reflection on God's word continually challenges my worldview as I confront the worldview of Jesus. It moves me from the cult of self to the call of servant. I can always tell the depth of my devotion by the content of my prayers. When my prayers are, "Help me accomplish…help me achieve," then my devotion is weak and shallow. As I come more to the place of, "Not my will, but yours be done," and "Lord, have mercy on me, a sinner," I am discovering again the deep places of my truest hunger and thirst.

A More Passionate Life *Purpose*

The practice of daily devotion renews the purpose in my life. The stronger and more compelling the "Why," the greater the creativity and energy. A big "Why" makes for uncompromisable integrity. This is why Jesus withdrew—to create a margin of devotion as the first act of his day. *"Very early in the morning, while it was still dark, Jesus got up, left the house and went off to a solitary place, where he prayed"* (Mark 1:35). Devotion was the first discipline of his day.

When I get up in the morning, I shave, shower, and dress before I leave the house. In the same way we must take the time to cleanse our spirits and dress our life visions before we begin the day's activities. I must take the time to renew God's "Why" in my life so that I attack the dawn by seeking meaning over money and by making a lasting contribution to the kingdom of God over personal accomplishment and achievement. The bigger the "Why," the greater the purpose will be.

I will not just settle for a job because God has given me a life calling. I will set out to build a life and not just a resume. This daily practice renewed the "Why" in Jesus' life and gave him the resolution to keep his focus set toward his ultimate God-given date with destiny on the cross in Jerusalem. He did not waver in the face of temptation nor abandon the mission in the frustration of fickle followers.

Devotion brings me back to my center. I am not the master of my day but the servant of God's purpose. My work is not the center of my journey, nor is ministry the center of my life; God is. My identity is that of a servant. In leadership, your privileges and rights decrease as your responsibility and influence increase. Jesus the Messiah didn't assume the head place at the table but assumed the servant position of washing feet. Working more, not less, has allowed many church leaders to have greater impact.

Twelve years ago we began doing a Saturday evening worship celebration in order to reach more people. Now with three Saturday celebrations we are able to reach over 1000 people who may have never felt comfortable in a Sunday morning celebration. Saturday is not a working day for the typical fifty-something with a graduate education, but it's not about me. I am not the master of my day but the servant of God's purpose.

Leadership is not about personal accomplishment and recognition. Leadership is about serving God by building people. It is not about us. We are servants of God Almighty doing only what God asks of us!

When you assume the kneeling posture of servant, you must look up to God. You are reminded that God is not a cosmic waiter at your beck and call, waiting to be motioned over to bless your latest business deal. God revealed himself to us through Jesus as servant, and we are most like God when we are serving.

The discipline of daily devotion reminds me of the frailty of my mortality. I realize that my time is short: I'm going to die! It creates a sense of urgency.

> *Now listen, you who say, "Today or tomorrow we will go to this or that city, spend a year there, carry on business and make money." Why, you do not even know what will happen tomorrow. **What is your life? You are a mist that appears for a little while and then vanishes**. Instead, you ought to say, "If it is the Lord's will, we will live and do this or that."* (James 4:13-15, emphasis added)

In the era after September 11, 2001 and the Asian tsunami of December 2004, we have a new awareness that our wealth cannot protect us. We've been reminded that no matter how technologically advanced or wealthy we become, we are not in control.

When the monster wave brought total destruction to thousands of towns, many of us became aware of what was really important. Wealthy tourists changed clothes, put on sweat pants, and went out into the debris to look for survivors. Others went back out to surf. They had been on vacation, and no tsunami was going to disrupt their plans. They were going to live and spend money as if no one was dying.

The devastation reminded me of Jesus' prediction of the last days:

> As it was in the days of Noah, so it will be at the coming of the
> Son of Man. For in the days before the flood, people were eating and
> drinking, marrying and giving in marriage, up to the day Noah
> entered the ark; and they knew nothing about what would happen
> until the flood came and took them all away. That is how it will be
> at the coming of the Son of Man. (Matt. 24:37-39)

Translation for today: "In the days before the flood, people were partying and surfing. They were surfing in the midst of floating corpses and debris. People consumed for their own selfish purposes and knew nothing about what was to come."

The practice of devotion renews the "Why" in my life. "_You do not even know what will happen tomorrow. What is your life? You are a mist that appears for a little while and then vanishes_" (James 4:14). We're not guaranteed tomorrow, and we must do the work of Christ who calls us while it is still today. "_Night is coming, when no one can work_" (John 9:4).

A More Passionate Life Practice

A daily life practice of being fully present to God's presence is the foundation of all other leadership disciplines. God speaks to those who are listening and wants to insure the success of God's purpose through those same people. The magi who came to Bethlehem to honor the birth of Jesus took the time to discern the voice of God and then went back by another road. Jesus' earthly father, Joseph, was able to elude danger and move his family to Egypt because he was listening to God's directive. The Bible records example after example of people who received vital directives from God that would help sustain personal health, integrity, and strategic focus for the duration of the journey.

God can speak to you today in a way that guides your daily practice. It begins with getting spiritually dressed for the day. Let me show you a specific way that I have discovered best connects me to God's presence and purpose each day.

F

1 SAMUEL

FRIDAY: THERE MAY BE GIANTS   3/4/05

God's promise of provision does not eliminate obstacles in our walk with him. However, God does provide deliverance as we face those challenges with determination and confidence in God, as David did. The "giants" in our lives will be overcome as we trust in God's power and provision.

SCRIPTURE

1 Samuel 17:1-58

OBSERVATIONS

- expect to go against champions!
- Goliath made a crazy wager, (all or nothing). No one is invinceable. Pride goes before the fall!!!
- Both sides were stuck in peacock procrastination & David got things rolling
- David ran to the battle lines! Man of action
- vs 32 - Leadership is out in front, always acting and not reacting.
- vs 34 - David applies skills he learned as shephard to skills he needs as warrior/leader.
- vs 37 - great faith!!!
- vs 39 - David doesn't try to fit into someone elses armour (style)

transformation journal

A ONE YEAR JOURNEY THROUGH THE BIBLE

NAME PERSONAL APPLICATIONS

"I come against you in the name of the Lord almighty . . . This day the Lord will deliver you into my hands . . . "

~ utter humility - forward action - total faith !!!

- my strength is not in my own ability or resources " it is not by sword or spear that the Lord saves, for the battle is the Lord's . . . "

- vs 50 " without a sword in his hand (David) struck down the Philistine and killed him "

- David's always "running" to the task of mission,

Prayer · Father, empower me to be today who you need me to me and to be who my family believes me to be

JOURNAL QUESTIONS

•What characteristics does David demonstrate in this trial? What benefits did David's faith bring to his community?

•What "giants" are you facing right now? What actions can you take that will model David's character as you address these obstacles?

Time in the *Transformation Journal:* How to Use the S.O.N. Study Method

I begin with prayer, asking God to open my heart and mind to new truths, to let me see today's Scripture through God's eyes, and to help me understand it with the heart and spirit of Jesus.

Next the **S**cripture. I read it carefully and find myself tuning in particularly to the leadership principles described and demonstrated in the text.

As I make **O**bservations about the Scripture, I often re-read portions of it and write down notes about what is happening in the text or story. I also make a note of questions or ideas I have, and insights into what God is doing or saying.

Last, I **N**ame the practical implications, taking a closer look at the observations and then applying them to my own life and context. I look for big principles God wants me to understand as well as simple spiritual truths that challenge me to grow. God often shows me specific steps to take that day in order to align my attitude and actions with God's vision for my life.

Many times I will sum up what I've learned in a prayer of repentance, or ask for wisdom and strength for the day ahead. I take time to pray specifically for people that God has put on my heart. God uses this time to give focus to my own personal life as well as to the strategic direction of the ministry I lead.

Devotion in Motion

God can't steer a parked car. God is looking for people who will take their lives out of park and shift them into drive.

How badly do you want it? John Wesley, the great evangelist who began the Methodist movement, talked about practical holiness, and "going on to perfection." You play a part in going on to (w)holiness and creating the movement of momentum in your life. So, grab that gearshift, take your life out of park, throw it into drive, and begin moving towards God's place of promise.

Momentum for Life Devotional

Read aloud the main Scriptures, Psalm 121 and 123.

1. What do those closest to you say is your passion?

2. When you "_lift up your eyes to the hills,_" what "god" offers you immediate relief in times of stress?

3. "God is looking for people who will take their lives out of park and shift them into drive." How does this statement apply to you?

4. What is one thing God is saying to you about your own devotion? Share your own action step.

CHAPTER THREE
Readiness for Lifelong Learning

READINESS> Prepared or available for service, action, or progress. Prompt willingness. i.e., "Readiness to resume study or continue discussions."

"In vain you rise early and stay up late, toiling for food to eat—for he grants sleep to those he loves."
(Ps. 127:2)

Work is a major component in our lives. Regardless of career choice or job location, we spend more time working than on any other single activity in our brief lifetimes. Most of us will spend more time at work this week than we will with our spouse, family, or friends. While you may get six to seven hours of sleep tonight, you will have worked eight to ten hours.

God desires to make the most of that time and intends for our work to have a purpose. It is not God's will that we toil in vain, anxious labor. Work is meant to be both fruitful and fulfilling. If we are not intentional about continual growth and improvement, we can spend our entire forty-plus-year career span like the men and women of Israel who walked aimlessly in the wilderness, never reaching their destiny or tasting the produce of promise.

Growth and fruitfulness go hand in hand. If I am not practicing a daily disciplined ascent in my life's work, then I will just keep on preaching the same old sermons, singing the same old songs, and writing the same old books—and my work will not be relevant, fulfilling, or fruitful.

Remember, our destination is the house of God, the temple of God. It was the only place a Jewish person could go to make an honorable, excellent offering. To continue to grow, there must be certain daily disciplines, or life practices, that we have in place to continue our ascent. Ascent is upward. Ascent never reaches a comfortable plane or plateau.

To maintain healthy forward momentum for life, I begin my day with a focused hour of **D**evotion—it is the first act of my day. Jesus reminds us that the most important commandment calls us to love God with all our *heart* (Matt. 22:37). "Heart" is about who I am at the core of my being. It is the part of me that affects all my thoughts, actions, and decisions. Who I am becoming in Jesus is the most important gift that I have and can offer back to God. It is my acceptable sacrifice.

This commandment also calls us to love God with all our *mind* (Matt. 22:37). Right after I spend about an hour listening to God (it takes me a long time, because I have a bend in my character), I spend at least a half-hour in the discipline or exercise of stretching my mind. This is the practice of lifelong learning. It means I'll never get out of school. I study everything from magazine articles and books to Web sites and newspapers. I read and study about leadership, business, technology, history, and religion. I am interested in church trends, cultural trends, and market trends. More importantly, I want to know how great leaders of the past stayed both faithful and fruitful.

> **We must sustain the never-out-of-school attitude of a child if we are to truly enter into the fruitfulness of kingdom living.**

Jesus told us that we must sustain the never-out-of-school attitude of a child if we are to truly enter into the fruitfulness of kingdom living (Mark 10:15). Children are constantly learning, so much so that their adult caretakers can get irritated with their incessant "Why?" "Why?" and more, "Why?"

Everything for a child is adventure. They can turn a bath into a Jacques Cousteau deep-sea excursion. They can find something interesting and new on every trip to the bus stop, even though they've covered the same path a hundred times. Simple objects, whether a kitchen utensil or a cardboard box, become cherished equipment for the task at hand.

What we call garbage, children call gold. My regular practice is to throw empty boxes out into my garage and then flatten them every Wednesday night to put into the recycling bin outside. When our children were younger, it wasn't unusual to come home from work and find those same boxes back inside the house, magically enjoying new lives as cars, forts, and spaceships. This is an incredible habit of childhood. Adults watch TV while children create.

Sometimes adults call this creativity "mischief." When I was a kid, my friends and I built a fort. We started out sawing down trees to make a log cabin, but soon discovered how much work that would entail, so we went around the neighborhood scavenging materials to use in constructing our fort. We took anything we could find to complete the project. Our fort even had a brick fireplace inside where we built fires!

We also had an arsenal of weapons. The fort sported an artillery slingshot I carved designs into, equipped with a rubber inner tube for firing our projectiles. It took one kid to hold the thing and another to pull it back. I remember one night I went home and my dad said, "Mrs. Carol called me and said that Bobby came home with a cut. His forehead was bleeding. Do you know anything about that?" I replied, "Yes, Dad, but I hit him on the move. It's not easy to hit a moving target—I should get points!"

We were creative, even in our mischief! We continued in our architectural pursuits for about two weeks until our parents made us tear down the fort, claiming it was a rattrap. So we moved on to another new adventure, another quest to explore, pioneer, innovate, and irritate. We kept asking, "Why?"

An Honorable, Excellent Offering

We no longer make the journey of ascent to the Temple of God to offer bulls, sheep, or doves. Instead, our *life work* becomes the honorable, excellent offering that we make to God. It is not about us; rather, our whole life work, regardless of what we do, is to become an honorable, excellent offering to God. The stretching of our minds allows our work to continue on the upward ascent of God's purpose.

> **Our whole life work, regardless of what we do, is to become an honorable, excellent offering to God.**

As I commit myself to this discipline, this practice of readiness for lifelong learning, then my work will be creative, redemptive, and innovative.

Creative Work

You were created to be creative. This is the work that Jesus wants to release in your life. It is what it means to be created in the image of God.

According to the opening pages of the Bible, God worked for six days and rested for one. God didn't party for six days and then work for one. Work is good! If it wasn't good, God would not have done it. Work is why we are here on planet Earth. After creating Adam, *"The LORD God took the man and put him in the Garden of Eden to work it and take care of it"* (Gen. 2:15). The implications here are powerful: You and I are co-workers; we are co-creators with God.

All work and all creativity begin in your mind. The physical manifestation of any reality begins as a mental thought. On a family picnic in 1959, a Dayton toolmaker named Ermal Fraze found he had no can opener. At that time, you had to use a tool called a church key to open a can of soda or beer, which was one of life's major annoyances that ruined many a family outing if the key had been forgotten. I still have my dad's church key, which was a pain to use. If you carried it in your pocket, it could rip your pants. It could also cut your hand.

Fraze knew there had to be a better way to open a can, and being a toolmaker, he suspected the solution had something to do with rivets. He ended up putting a rivet on top of the can to create a pull-tab. Within a few years he invented, patented, and began manufacturing the "easy open" pull-tab lid that is now standard equipment. Today Fraze Pavilion, a popular outdoor entertainment venue in Kettering, Ohio, is named after Fraze, an inventor with an idea that began in his head.

You must conceive it before you can achieve it. It is why the Bible talks to us about renewing our minds (Rom. 12:1-2). To renew my mind means I must stretch it.

To renew my mind means I must stretch it.

In the beginning was the Word, and the Word was with God, and the Word was God. He was with God in the beginning. Through him all things were made. (John 1:1-2)

The first chapter of the Gospel of John tells us that the Logos, or divine intellect of God, became flesh. We know the Logos as Jesus. *"The Word became flesh and made his dwelling among us"* (John 1:14). In the mind of God an idea was conceived, and the thoughts became reality.

Like God, we must conceive before we can achieve. When Beethoven wrote the Ninth Symphony, he was totally deaf. Most people think music comes from what our ears hear, but in reality we must think it first. The symphony was first formed in Beethoven's mind. He "heard" it in his mind, and the idea was created into physical reality. All physical creation begins first as a mental thought.

Pursuit of Wisdom

The Bible repeatedly challenges us to pursue wisdom. Wisdom requires bigger thinking. Wisdom requires new thinking. Wisdom requires the exercise of a person's mind. God cannot use narrow-minded people, close-minded people, or empty-minded people. Jesus said that you can't put new wine into old wineskins (Matt. 9:17). Old wineskins have lost their ability to stretch.

I hate the discipline of stretching before my physical workouts. I'm tempted to cheat and not do it, but if I don't stretch, I will lose flexibility. God is a God of new things, calling us to sing a new song. God is looking for people with flexible minds that can receive new ideas and for people who will let those ideas be manifested into physical reality. God will not trust the valued, aged wine of redemptive wisdom to minds that are not subject to the practice of stretching, the daily discipline of renewed thinking.

God will not trust the valued, aged wine of redemptive wisdom to minds that are not subject to the daily discipline of renewed thinking.

God is no respecter of persons. God is not looking around and saying, "Okay, I like Mike better, so I am going to choose Mike for my next new idea." If you are not stretching your mind, however, God is not going to waste new wine by putting it into old skins. The obstacle to forward momentum is old thinking. Making strategic plans from old paradigms is a recipe for bursting wineskins. Old wineskins will burst because they have lost their ability to be flexible. Remember those deadly words: "We never did it that way before." When I am stretching my mind, I am always looking forward to the next new thing.

My grandfather was challenged by the myriad of changes going on in the world around his eighty-something-year-old paradigms. He marveled on one occasion that I could speak at Ginghamsburg Church (outside Dayton, Ohio) on a Sunday morning and at 8:00 PM that same night could be in Pasadena, California, speaking to an entirely different group of people. It was beyond my grandfather's comprehension. Years later, up to the time he died, he'd ask, "Did you really do that?"

My grandfather was working from an old mental paradigm, a horse-and-buggy way of thinking. That's how he grew up. He saw his first automobile at age sixteen and bought one at age twenty-two, an incredible paradigm shift for him. He told me about his horse named Prince pulling the buggy for his date and himself. He'd drop off his date at her home, fall asleep at the reigns, and wake up at his farm gate because Prince knew the way back. (Try that with a car!) Little did my grandfather realize that as he was going about his daily affairs in a horse cart, Orville and Wilbur Wright—sons of a bishop in Dayton, Ohio—were stretching their paradigms about a new means and mode of travel that would make possible my cross-continent, same-day schedule.

My grandfather had never been on an airplane when he died in 1996. Neither his horse nor a car could get me to California in one afternoon. That kind of travel required a shift of thinking.

The same mind-stretching was required with the invention of the cell phone. It has dramatically changed our lives at home, at school, at work, and on vacation—in approximately ten years! Until the cell phone, my telephone number was tied to a physical address. You would look up my name in a telephone book, and you would read my address and then my telephone number. You could not separate a telephone number from a physical address. Yet when I was speaking in the mountains in the Czech Republic, three hours from Prague, I could take my cell phone out of my pocket and call my son in Kansas City to ask how his baseball game went. That's a paradigm shift.

Many of God's children let their minds atrophy. God is looking for people who are willing to exercise their minds, to be transformed by their renewing. I have the living presence of Christ dwelling within me. Jesus said that we would **Many of God's children let their minds atrophy.** be able to do the things that he did and to do even greater things (John 14:12). All things are possible with God, but God will not trust his redemptive work to inflexible spirits or minds.

The discipline of daily reading is work. Stretching hurts. Many people tell me, "I don't like to read." Hebrews 12:11 says, *"No discipline seems pleasant at the time, but painful. Later on, however, it produces a harvest of righteousness and peace for those who have been trained by it."* In other words, discipline requires sweat equity, but the benefits of discipline reap a bountiful payoff. You could say the benefits are out of this world!

A God of Excellence

The sister of creativity is excellence. God worked six days, and at the end of every day said, "That was good!" However at the end of the sixth day God said, "That was *very* good!" God did not stop working when it was good. God did not cease working until it was *very* good (Gen. 1:31). God is a God of excellence.

When we are committed to excellence, it honors God and builds strong self-esteem. One of the greatest needs I see in the life of the Church is self-esteem, and when we are able to offer God our best, the result is healthy esteem. Psalm 127:2 says, "*He grants sleep to those he loves.*" This implies that fruitful, excellent labor results in restful sleep. When our work reflects the excellence of God, we get to the end of the day and just want to high-five God, saying, "We did good today, God!" We can go to sleep at night knowing that we are getting an incredible return on our investment. This partnership affords us a strong sense of contribution, personal worth, and satisfaction.

Excellence is not about comparing ourselves or our work with the work of others. You don't look around and say, "I am doing better than that person." We have a higher standard. The company doesn't set our standard. The union doesn't determine the pace of our work. We work by God's standards.

When I speak at conferences, people ask me which one of my books is my best one. I always reply, "I haven't written my best book yet." I haven't preached my best sermon yet, I haven't sung my best song yet, and I haven't made my best offering to God yet. From a biblical perspective, the best is yet to come. I am on a journey of ascent. I am always looking up. The sense of focus comes from my discipline of lifelong learning every day, and the best is yet to come.

God always saves the best for last. Remember Jesus' first water-to-wine miracle? Most party hosts served the best wine first and then brought the inferior product out when everyone was a little tipsy and couldn't tell the difference. Not so with Jesus. "*You have saved the best until now*" (John 2:10). This is what the journey of ascent is about. It just keeps getting better. Even the prospect of death is no threat, for the best is yet to come.

I don't want to get old, but I do want to become aged like good wine. There is a difference. We all have God-dreams for our education, careers, and marriages, yet many people I know give up on those dreams by the time they're thirty. They begin to grow prematurely old in their minds and spirits, losing the ability to stay fresh and flexible in the ascent. By age fifty they want to retire. Retirement is not a biblical option. It is the consequence of people losing their God-inspired momentum.

Retirement is not a biblical option. It is the consequence of people losing their God-inspired momentum.

Moses, a lifelong learner himself, wasn't even ripe for God's picking until he was eighty years old. At the full-bodied age of eighty, he had grown sufficiently in spirit and in wisdom to maximize the fruitfulness of his leadership.

Many people quit before they realize their most productive years of service. God's best is yet to come! Consider these lifelong learners:

- Michelangelo, at the age of fifty-nine, learned a new method of painting upside down, and painted *The Last Judgment* on the ceiling of the Sistine Chapel.

- At age sixty-six Colonel Harland Sanders started the Kentucky Fried Chicken chain.

- At age sixty-nine Ronald Reagan was elected to his first term as president, the oldest person to be elected president until he topped his own record and was reelected at seventy-three.

- Golda Meir became prime minister of Israel at age seventy-one.

- Nelson Mandela became the first black president of South Africa at the age of seventy-five after being a political prisoner for twenty-seven years.

- John Glenn, at the age of seventy-seven, made his second trip into outer space.

- At age eighty-one, Benjamin Franklin was elected as a delegate to the U.S. Constitutional Convention, leading our country on a very different course from what would have occurred without his participation.

- Well into his eighties, Paul Harvey continues to get up every morning to record his daily radio broadcast heard around the globe.

- At the age of one hundred Strom Thurmond completed his eighth term as a U.S. Senator.

Just as these leaders were all lifelong learners, you and I must never leave school. We must each practice the daily discipline of lifelong learning. We must hold onto the inquisitive nature of the child within so that we don't miss the incredible wonders of the kingdom of God. Mediocrity does not honor God.

Mediocrity does not honor God.

I love Jesus' demonstration of excellence when he healed the blind man of Bethesda (Mark 8:22-25). Jesus spat, rubbed his spit into the man's eyes, and then asked, in essence, "Well, how is it?" The blind man replied, "I can see colors and movement, but everything is kind of blurry. People look like they are trees walking around, but it's okay—really!"

Jesus said, "Hold on. We are not into 'okay' here. Let's give it another go-around." Jesus touched him once more, and the job was complete—20/20 vision. Jesus didn't quit until the job was done, and done with excellence. Jesus wasn't into mediocrity, and to bear the name of Jesus requires that we pursue the excellence of God as well. It doesn't get any better than when your time to die comes, and you are able to say to the Father, "I have finished with excellence the work you sent me to do."

Redemptive Work

How many hours will you spend doing your job this week? The majority of us will put in a minimum of forty hours with many of us working fifty hours and beyond.

What is the purpose of work from God's perspective? Work is an act of worship. *"Therefore, I urge you, brothers and sisters, in view of God's mercy, to offer your bodies as a living sacrifice, holy and pleasing to God—this is true worship"* (Rom. 12:1). The Greek word for *worship* is the same word used for service. Some Bibles translate *worship* here as work. To worship is to render physical service. Your work is your spiritual service to God. To work is to worship, and to worship is to work; it's bringing an honorable, excellent offering to God.

Our culture has reduced the idea of worship to a one-hour, weekly event, when it is really a daily endeavor of all our work. The word *liturgy* comes from two Greek words: *laos* (people) and *ergon* (work). Liturgy means people at work.

The motive of our work is to render service to God. It means to be a daily part of God's redemptive work in the world. That is the whole reason why we work.

The Psalms of Ascent remind us of the potential distractions and idolatries that can take us off path and keep us from reaching the ultimate purpose of God for our lives. Psalm 127 calls our attention to the perils of vain labor. One of the things that can knock you off the journey God has for your life is "vain labor" or fruitless work. Vain work or futile work is any work you do that is not part of God's redemptive work in the world.

What makes the difference? It is futile work if you, rather than God, are at the center. It is "in vain" when the motive of our work is driven by money. Jesus called this the bigger-barns syndrome. He told the story of a man whose entire motive for working was to make money. After he made a lot of money, he still couldn't see beyond himself as the center of the universe. *"He said, 'This is what I'll do. I will tear down my barns and build bigger ones, and there I will store my surplus grain. And I'll say to myself,*

"You have plenty of grain laid up for many years. Take life easy; eat, drink and be merry"'" (Luke 12:18-19).

Jesus called that man a fool, and later said, *"Do not work for food that spoils, but for food that endures to eternal life, which the Son of Man will give you"* (John 6:27).

Not long ago I spoke with a businessman in his forties, living in our community, and working in the field of engineering. "You know what I always wanted to do with my life?" he remarked to me. "I always wanted to teach at a community college. That is my ultimate goal. When I retire, I'm going to teach at a community college."

I replied, "You mean, if you could do anything in the world right now, you would teach at a community college?"

"Yes," he said.

"Why are waiting until you retire? You could die in a year— who knows when you're going to die? Why don't you just go do it now? You have a Master's degree; just go teach in a community college."

You know what he said to me? "I can't afford to."

When my work is driven by the monetary return on my labors, then I am really saying, "My security comes from money, not God's promise of provision." When we do this, we become fearful to do what God has placed in our heart or to risk the passion that God has poured into our heart. I believe in God, but I trust money for my security. That's today's version of the bigger-barns syndrome.

When I went into ministry, my first salary was $3,800 a year. Both my parents and Carolyn's parents said, "You're crazy." Carolyn's dad, who was a Christian, said, "Well, you have a great heart, Mike, but how are you going to feed my grandbabies?"

Amazingly, I poured myself into the passion God placed in my heart, and the blessings God provided for me have potentially surpassed what I would have made in the business world.

Why do so many of us profess our belief in God but trust money for our security? Faith is the ultimate expression of the object of your trust. We've only been given this one life. To waste that life because money is the source of your well-being and provision is vain worship. Many people master the art of *making* a living but never discover the *joy* of living.

> **Many people master the art of making a living but never discover the joy of living.**

Life is too short to work at a job only for the purpose of earning a living. I want a life calling, not a job. I want to build a *life*—not a resume! God has placed a great passion in your heart. Pursue that passion with everything that you profess, and trust God's provision.

As I write this chapter, I am reading the book *The Smartest Guys in the Room* by Bethany McLean and Peter Elkind. It profiles Kenneth Lay, who was the founder and CEO of Enron, the fifth-biggest company in the world. Enron went belly-up and took all the employees' retirement money. The authors describe Lay as a person of *intended* integrity. "Lay seemed to care deeply about bettering the world. He spent much of his time on philanthropy: in Houston, he was the go-to man for charitable works, raising and giving away millions. He spoke often about corporate values. And he was openly religious. 'Everybody knows that I personally have a very strict code of personal conduct that I live by,' he once told an interviewer for a religious magazine called *The Door*. 'This code is based on Christian values.'"[12]

How could a man who apparently held such high standards destroy the trust of thousands of employees and investors and send a quake through the world's economy? Jesus said that none of us is able to serve two masters (Matt. 6:24). You cannot work for both God and money. Somewhere along the way Mr. Lay got distracted by the idol of "vain labor." The quest for more money became the mantra driving the meaning of his journey of ascent. When Lay discovered that the two people who led one of Enron's divisions were engaging in criminal acts, he refused to fire them. According to McLean and Elkind, Kenneth Lay stated openly at a company board meeting that these directors made too much money for the company to let them go.[13]

Kenneth Lay seemed to be working "for food that spoils." The measure of work is not the wealth it produces for us, but the opportunities that it provides for service. Our work becomes an honorable, excellent offering to God as we contribute to the well-being of others. This is true worship!

The Priority of People

We work for the benefit of others. One of the Psalms of Ascent reminds us of the motivation for this life journey. *"For the sake of my friends and of all the people, I will say, 'Peace be within you.' For the sake of the house of the LORD our God, I will seek your prosperity"* (Psalm 122:8-9).

The gospel is counter to the many of the cultural values portrayed in reality programs such as *The Apprentice* and *Survivor*, where the goal is to gain advantage and ultimate victory over your teammates. Work must never exploit people for the purpose of personal profit or self-gain.

When I am actively participating in the redemptive work of Jesus, then my labors will add value, enhance quality of life, and promote connectedness in relationship. When my work is not an act of worship, it will result in the construction of a tower of Babel. *"Then they said to each other, 'Come, let us build ourselves a city, with a tower that reaches to the heavens, so that we may make a name for ourselves'"* (Gen. 11:4). While bigger barns are all about more money, towers of Babel are all about more me. My achievement, my recognition, and my personal success become the driving, motivating force behind my work, rather than making a lasting contribution to God's greater redemptive purpose.

Ross is a Jesus-follower and a passionate car salesperson whose sales record is always near the top at the dealership where he works. Now here's the paradox: several years ago he refused to sell me a car that I would have used credit to buy. Ross was convinced the acquisition would have overstretched my financial well-being. He truly seeks the prosperity of others, as the psalmist describes.

People like Ross have power with God by their actions toward people. As I emphasized in the previous chapter, whatever we do or fail to do for people, we do or fail to do for God. We want to be among the ones that Jesus welcomes with great reward: "*Come, you who are blessed by my Father; take your inheritance, the kingdom prepared for you since the creation of the world*" (Matt. 25:34). It's as we respond to people's true needs, whether hunger, thirst, homelessness, sickness, or even financial imprisonment, that we truly serve the God we name.

Worship is the honorable, excellent offering you're making to God through your work as part of God's redemptive purpose in the world.

We're all going to die, and the offering we make to God is all that will live beyond us. Your worship is far more than the songs you sing in church. Worship is the honorable, excellent offering you're making to God through your work as part of God's redemptive purpose in the world.

A Poured-Out Sacrament

When we daily offer our work to God as an action of worship, then God makes our work a poured-out sacrament in the lives of others around us. "*Whoever finds their life will lose it, and whoever loses their life for my sake will find it*" (Matt. 10:39). The greater the sacrifice we are willing to make, the broader the scope of influence that God will allow us to have in the lives of other people.

The greater the sacrifice we are willing to make, the broader the scope of influence that God will allow us to have.

The practice of going to work every day provides the opportunity for you to be a poured-out sacrament in the lives of other people. When I place myself in God's hands, God is able to use my offering as squeezed-out grapes and broken bread, sustenance in the lives of other people.

When I began preaching at worship celebrations on Saturday night, it really wasn't a terribly difficult choice, even though I previously had both Mondays and Saturdays off. Nobody told me I

83

had to start working on Saturdays. The idea came when I prayed, "How much more of a blessing could I be in this short lifetime if I am willing to work on Saturdays?" My income didn't change when I started working Saturdays, but I was able to be a greater influence for God. That was a sacrifice I was willing to make. In the hands of Jesus, I become a sacrament in the lives of other people.

For me, the harder decision was not the initial one of launching a Saturday-night celebration. The key is *staying* in the hand of God on a daily basis, and that's not as easy as it sounds. When I fail to stay available to God by neglecting to practice my daily disciplines, then I become more like a marble than a grape, inflexible and void of anything to offer others. You just can't squeeze life out of a marble.

The disciplined, daily practice of lifelong learning makes me more useful in God's service to others. Gordon McDonald reminds us, "The development of the mind makes it possible for men and women to be servants to the generation in which they live."[14]

Do you know why God chose Moses? Even at eighty years old, Moses was a lifelong learner. Moses was strategic to God's purpose because he was a lifelong student of his culture and time. "*Moses was educated in all the wisdom of the Egyptians and was powerful in speech and action*" (Acts 7:22). We must begin our day by stretching our spirit in reflective study and active listening through God's word. And like Moses, we must then stretch our minds through the study of the ideas, mores, and preferences of the cultures in which we live and work, positioning ourselves to make the most honorable, excellent offering to God possible.

Innovative Work

It is amazing to note Jesus' methods of innovation as he went about doing the work of God. "*Having said this, he spit on the ground, made some mud with the saliva, and put it on the man's eyes. 'Go,' he told him, 'wash in the Pool of Siloam.' ... So the man went and washed, and came home seeing*" (John 9:6-7). In Kim Miller's book *Designing Worship* (Group Publishing, 2004) she asks, "What does it take to make a miracle happen? From our own limited perspectives, we imagine God with sparkling magic potions carefully arranged in a heavenly toolbox. Maybe with a few wands thrown in for the really tough jobs. God's best work, however, has always been done with amazingly ordinary stuff—water, mud, spit, a piece of stale bread, a barn, a teenage girl, twelve dysfunctional disciples. God uses ordinary objects in regular places with everyday people."[15]

During America's industrial age Dayton, Ohio was known as a center of innovation. From its poets (Paul Laurence Dunbar) to its pilots (the Wright brothers), Dayton looked to the future. Consider these inventors:

- Ermal Fraze: Pull-top beverage cans (profiled earlier in this chapter)
- William Church: Cellophane tape
- Charles Kettering: Electric automobile starter
- C. Francis Jenkins: Movie projector, movie camera, movie film, and theater
- James Ritty: Cash register
- Floyd Smith: Parachute
- Albert Smith: Computing scale for butchers and grocers.

Our world is constantly changing, and God is continually creating new wine. You can't put new wine into yesterday's wineskins. An economic report released in early 2005 reported Ohio as being next-to-last in the rankings of states that are creating new jobs (Michigan was last). Ohio and Michigan's economies are dependent on the industries that support Detroit and the automobile industry. The area once known as the industrial belt for its mastery of the industrial age is now referred to as the rust belt because we have not yet figured how to make the transition to the technological age of information.

Compare that situation to the church that has not made the transition from an age that valued traditional rural-family-based values to an age that prefers pop-urban-individual-based values. Mark Driscoll, a young pastor in Seattle, effectively makes the case for continual innovation in his book, *The Radical Reformission*: "Churches have to continually examine and adjust their musical styles, websites, aesthetics, acoustics, programming, and just about everything but their Bible in an effort to effectively communicate the gospel to as many people as possible in the cultures around them."[16]

When you quit growing, you quit being useful to God. When you quit stretching your spirit and your mind, you plateau. You leave the path of ascent, and your life and work will be neither fulfilling nor fruitful.

People who are committed to the lifelong discipline of learning continue to add value to the endeavors that they are committed to. Most folks can readily identify the obstacles and problems that are inherent to any organization. Take, for example, the twelve spies Moses sent out as advance scouts into the Promised Land. Ten members of the board readily identified all the "why we can't" barriers, but Joshua and Caleb were able to find the "why we can" solutions and lead the way.

I will never put anyone who is not committed to a rugged discipline of lifelong learning on our staff or church board. Everyone I work with must be committed to becoming an expert in God's future. The senior management team and leadership board of our church travel together around the country to study the best innovative practices of other ministries.

Your Own Practice of Lifelong Learning

Consider these three practices of lifelong learning: reading, observing, and doing.

Read

First, you should always be reading something. I ask people who are successful and faithful what they are reading. If people are moving forward on the journey of ascent, I want to know what they are reading.

I asked Bill Weikert, the chair of our board and a co-owner of a local company, what he was reading. He told me he was reading *The Smartest Guys in the Room*, which is about the Enron scandal. He told me I ought to read it, so that's why I got the book. As you can tell from my comments in this chapter, I didn't just buy the book, I read it and learned from it!

I want to move with people who are moving. You must always be reading something and must always be ready to share with someone what you are reading and how it is helping you become better.

Observe

Second, train yourself to observe. The Bible says wisdom cries aloud from the streets (Prov. 1:20). I am observing all the time, seeking for opportunities to learn. I am looking for pioneers, older people who are ahead of me making an honorable, excellent offering to God.

A lot of people start out as pioneers until life becomes a little dangerous. That is how Pittsburgh was founded. Lots of people in those posh, big, civilized Eastern cities like Boston and Philadelphia proclaimed, 'We're going west!' They got as far as Pittsburgh only to discover that Ohio was already occupied by people who were not excited about sharing the land. The going would be dangerous from there on out, and the pioneers quickly became settlers as they realized the cost involved.

I am not attracted to settlers. I'm observing older people who are faithfully continuing the ascent ahead of me. I'm watching for younger people who show signs of budding innovation. I am observing the best leaders and communicators in multiple venues.

When God called me to be a preacher, I didn't study preachers. I saw too much mediocrity there. I studied effective comedians! Richard Pryor and Bill Cosby were two of my mentors in communication skills. I figured that anyone who could talk for an hour and have people pay $75 a head to hear them had to have something going on. I considered it a compliment when someone said, "You remind me of a white Richard Pryor."

Anytime I have an opportunity to watch a comedy special on TV, I watch it and study everything the comedian does. It's not that I want to be funny; I simply want to learn more about engaging an audience.

The Bible tells us to take the good and separate the bad (Matt. 10:16; 13:24-30), so I am continually observing the people who are great leaders and communicators. Name your circle of observation. These people become part of your mentoring network. Who are the great leaders and strong communicators that you can learn from?

Do

We learn the most from hands-on experience. We retain the most of what we read, see, and hear when we are able to practice by doing.

I am on a major learning curve even as I write this book. All the books I have previously written were inked out by hand on yellow legal pads. I wrote *Out on the Edge* (Abingdon Press, 1998)[17] in the 1990s about media and worship. It was one of the first Christian books with an accompanying interactive CD-ROM. The *Wall Street Journal* did a whole-page story on that book and Ginghamsburg's experience as a multi-media, multi-sensory church.[18] Yet look at the irony: I wrote a book about ministry entering the media age, but I used longhand on a yellow legal pad!

I am writing my newest book on a computer for the first time. I have never processed words before, but we learn by doing, and I am committed to the challenging, albeit often painful, discipline of relearning how to "write." I am fifty-three years old, but I am a baby in light of the potential for my thinking.

"No discipline seems pleasant at the time, but painful. Later on, however, it produces a harvest of righteousness and peace for those who have been trained by it" (Heb. 12:11). In other words, discipline is painful for a while, but it has one heaven of a payoff!

What will you do today to develop further your own discipline of lifelong learning? You've got only one life that will last but a few years on this earth. That life was created to be an honorable, excellent offering to God, and the greatest expression of worship is your work. Commit yourself every day to the practice of learning and keep moving forward on your journey of ascent.

Momentum for Life Devotional

Read aloud the main Scripture, Psalm 127.

1. God desires our "work" to be fruitful and fulfilling, but we aren't all experiencing this benefit. How would you describe your work/day job?
   • Just a paycheck
   • More frustrating than fulfilling
   • Enjoyable, but I don't see how it's fruitful for God
   • Fruitful and fulfilling

2. What would change if you started seeing all your work as worship?

3. Our work should always add value to the lives of others. How do you see your work adding value?

4. What do you hear God saying to you (so far) as you build momentum for life?

CHAPTER FOUR
Investing in Key Relationships

RELATIONSHIP> The state of being related; the mutual exchange between two people or groups who have dealings with one another; kinship.

> *"Your wife will be like a fruitful vine within your house; your children will be like olive shoots around your table. Yes, this will be the blessing for the man who fears the LORD." (Ps. 128:3-4)*

I can't remember the last time I cried.

Like many stoic men, I usually find myself holding my emotions in check as I keep my eyes focused straight ahead on the task at hand. I feel a certain responsibility as a husband, father, son, and pastor to do what I have to do and process it later. This compartmentalization usually works for me, but I experienced a week that required an exception to my norm.

It started one night with a 12:45 AM phone call from my sister in Cincinnati. "Dad just drove himself to the hospital," Gayle relayed. "He had chest pains, his blood pressure was 212/110, and they might have to do emergency surgery in two hours." So by 1:05 AM, I was racing down I-75 towards Cincinnati. A half-hour later I arrived at the hospital, where Gayle and I would keep vigil through the night.

Dad ended up not needing emergency surgery, yet seeing my eighty-year-old father lying anxious and confused in that hospital bed was extremely difficult for us. We remembered how just a few months before, he had driven from Florida to Ohio in a day.

Even more difficult were the doctor's words about the low survival rates of the various surgeries being considered for him. I began to think of things I would say at his funeral.

Still, I did not cry. "I will do whatever I have to do!" I told myself.

Later that same day, I went on our church's men's retreat. I had helped plan it and was also scheduled to speak to the men. It was Friday evening, and I was in the hotel room, hanging out with our teaching pastor Mike Bowie and guest speaker Rudy Rasmus from Houston, Texas, when my cell phone rang.

"Where are you?" my wife's voice broke on the other end.

My first thought was that something happened to my Dad. Carolyn began to cry hysterically. Mike and Rudy could hear her deep anguish over the phone. Not knowing what was wrong, they began to pray.

"Toby's dead!" Carolyn finally blurted out. Toby was our miniature schnauzer who was just four months shy of sixteen years old. I had given him to Carolyn for one of her significant birthdays. She had told me that he was the best present that I had ever given her. In recent months Toby had suffered some blindness and various older-dog maladies, but was still a cherished companion in our empty human nest.

"He's dead, Michael!" Carolyn continued. "I let him out into the backyard for a few minutes, and he didn't come in. I went out into the snow and found him lifeless in the fishpond."

Toby represents many different transitions and memories in my family's collective history. He was around when my grandparents were still alive. He was the family pet of our children's years at home, children now grown and living in different parts of the country. He was our faithful companion whose image marks the photographs of sacred family passages and memorable Christmas pasts. He sat next to me as I wrote each one of my books in our navy blue leather chair.

Quickly explaining to Mike and Rudy what had happened, I grabbed my luggage, threw it in my car, and headed for home. No time to truly feel my emotions—only the urgency to be who I need to be for Carolyn and for the care of the dog. I knew the drill: "I will do what I have to do…for my wife, for Toby, for the family." During the thirty-five-minute drive from the retreat site to home, my mind was racing. "It's February in Ohio. I need to do something with the dog tonight. How can I dig a burial hole in the frozen ground?" I tried to push away visions of Toby paddling helplessly in the water and then drowning—things a good dad should never allow to happen.

My thoughts weren't clear and orderly, more like flashes that swirled around my mind. Through the blur, I was aware of my deep sense of responsibility: "I will be who I have to be. I will do what I have to do. I am strong. I am a husband… dad… man… pastor… leader."

My dad's hospitalization, which had unfolded less than twenty-four hours previously, had left me feeling numb. I continued to experience that numbness even as I drove home.

I'll always remember the picture of what happened next. I walked through the door and saw Carolyn sitting on the couch in the family room. She held Toby, cradled in his blanket, on her lap.

That's when I lost it. I held our dead dog and nuzzled his ear, and I began to cry. It was a long, deep, painful mourning. A tidal wave of emotion gushed out at once. I felt an all-encompassing, gut-wrenching pain—the kind of pain I imagine people in my church experience over a child's death, cancer, abusive relationships, or addictions—feelings I typically insulate myself from. I agonized over the senseless deaths that result from murderous terrorist attacks and the quarter-million people who were washed away in the December 2004 tsunami. Grief-stricken, I got in touch with my own human condition of helplessness as I cried, "Why God? Why?"

Meaning and Relationships

We learn life and faith through the experience of family and friends.

The crisis of sickness and death is the ultimate reminder of life's true meaning. What is this life all about? What really matters? We are created for relationships. We learn life and faith through the experience of family and friends.

Relationship Rituals

We experience life through a pattern of relationship rituals. The rituals are different for each of us. Have you ever paused to consider the rituals that frame the relationships in your own extended family? I remember riding in the car every Sunday to my grandparents' house for lunch. My uncle's family was usually there too. I can still picture the seating arrangement in that crowded back-porch-turned-year-round-dining room of my grandparent's home. My grandfather was always at one end of the red-checked plastic tablecloth and my dad at the other. I sat next to Granddaddy and across from Uncle Thomas. In 1996 when my grandfather died, holiday meals found me in his former seat, with my father still at his post on the other end of the table.

Listening to the tribal stories around the table, I learned my identity. Through our relationship rituals, values were transmitted from one generation to another. I heard stories of faith at that table. My grandmother taught me my first Bible verse, John 3:16, at that table. As a very young child I was sitting at that table when I first met a person of another race, a Japanese seminary student. We played board games as a family around that table. I learned political ideology in the midst of heated debates around that table.

The family table is where I discovered the sacrament of life.

I experienced good and bad, function and dysfunction. Most of all I learned that God loved the world of people—all the people that I had experienced and talked about at that table. Through the relationships around that table, God's love took human form. The family table is where I discovered the sacrament of life.

While holiday meals can easily make a person sleepy, each passing year I'm less tempted to lose out on the precious time those meaningful holiday moments afford. I force myself to stay awake and look around, remembering that nothing will last forever. I want to breathe in the awe and wonder of my children interacting with their grandparents. I don't want to miss the experiences of relationships while I'm living in the middle of them.

We miss out on life and meaning if we are not making relationships a priority on any given day. People are created for relationships, and it's in the context of our relationship rituals that meaning is found.

We miss out on life and meaning if we are not making relationships a priority on any given day.

The Value of Life

I can't control life. I can't even control what happens in my own backyard! I want to think that I can always make my family safe, but look what happened to my beloved pet. I am still dealing with feelings of guilt over my own responsibility: Why did I install the fishpond last year? Why didn't I put a fence around it?

I'm facing the age-old life-question of Job: Why do bad things happen to good people? The day after my meltdown, I read about Moses' death and the grief of the Hebrew community, and I wrote in my journal, "Maybe death is what makes life so valuable!"

Life repeatedly informs us that we are not in control. The events that surrounded September 11, 2001 and the Asian tsunami in December 2004 remind us that no matter how far advanced we become in technology or how wealthy America is as a first-world nation, we cannot control the aging of a human life, the actions of other people, or the groaning of the earth. Our wealth and technology ultimately cannot protect or save us.

People Matter

Life is not about stuff we own or accumulate. It is not even about our personal accomplishment. Life is about people. Jesus said that whatever we do or fail to do for others, we do to him (Matt. 25:31-46). We can replace stuff, but we can't replace people!

Carolyn repeatedly asked herself the question, "Would I have done anything different in the weeks before Toby died?" Her answer is, "I would have held him more."

Carolyn takes her life's work very seriously, thus was working on the computer in an upstairs bedroom of our home that recent fateful night. She sent a last email at 9:27 PM and went downstairs to let Toby out. Her plan was to hold him in his blanket and warm him up when he came inside—but he never came back.

Life is not about our accumulated stuff or personal accomplishment. Life is about people.

Her thought about spending more time to hold Toby led Carolyn to other thoughts as she reflected later in the week. "Here's the question it makes me ask," she said. "Am I spending enough time with my mother?" Carolyn had not seen her eighty-five-year-old mother in two months. Toby's death had served as a sobering reminder of life's true meaning.

Margins

In Psalm 128 (another Psalm of Ascent), notice the integration of work and relationships as an expression of worship. "*Blessed are all who fear the LORD, who walk in obedience to him,*" it begins (v. 1). D-R-I-V-E begins with devotion to God. Every day, "devotion" is my act of getting in touch with God. What happens as a result? "*You will eat the fruit of your labor; blessings and prosperity will be yours*" (v. 2). When you fear the Lord, your work will become an honorable, excellent offering to God.

The psalm now moves from work to relationships. The two don't compete against each other, but complement. "*Your wife will be like a fruitful vine within your house; your children will be like olive shoots around your table. Yes, this will be the blessing for the man who fears the Lord"* (v.3-4).

When the object of our devotion is right, then our work and relationships combine together as an honorable, excellent offering to God. Think of the amount of energy we spend in work and relationships each week. God is not nearly as interested in the little religious ceremonies we call worship services. Our work and our relationships are not separate from our relationship with God but are the primary expressions of this relationship. They are the truest demonstrations of our worship.

Our work and our relationships are the truest demonstrations of our worship.

Do you want to honor God—to bring an honorable, excellent offering? We do this by creating and maintaining margins for the key relationships in our lives. On a piece of paper, the margin is that side thing—the empty space. Margins in life are the blank spaces on our calendars—our sacred spaces. You dare not allow your margin for relationships to fill up. When we keep open spaces and time for relationships, we honor God.

Isaiah 5:8 says, *"Ah, you who join house to house, who add field to field, until there is room for no one but you, and you are left to live alone in the midst of the land!"* (NRSV). In other words, all you do is work. You are consumed in real-estate transactions (joining house to house). You burn the candle at both ends to ensure a good harvest for your fields.

We are created for relationships, and relationships are developed in the margins of our lives. Acts of kindness are done in the margins. When you don't have any margins,

Relationships are developed in the margins of our lives.

people leave you alone because you are always on the edge.

Trouble in the Margins

We get into trouble when we allow our work to fill the margins that are meant for our relationships. That's what happened to

Carolyn and me. We allowed ministry to become a priority over our relationship, so that after twenty years of marriage we looked at each other and didn't know one another, let alone like each other! The problem was that we had allowed zero daily margins for our relationship.

In our youth, we discover that it is easier to focus on a task that can't scream at us and say, "You aren't meeting my needs!"

This is a mistake of youth. Many people fall into it, as did Carolyn and I.

Unfortunately too many of us don't figure out the problem until we are forty or fifty. Some never get it. In our youth, we discover that it is easier to focus on a task that can't scream at us and say, "You aren't meeting my needs!" Tasks reward us without talking back. Without realizing it, we learn to focus on tasks rather than relationships.

Here's how it begins. When you are dating, you are focused on building a relationship. You are finding out what pleases the other person. You explore what the other person likes and dislikes, and you listen to the deepest needs of their heart.

Next you become engaged. At that point you no longer focus on the relationship; you begin to center on the task of the wedding. The details of the wedding begin to swallow up valuable energy formerly invested in the relationship. When Carolyn and I became engaged, we were no longer listening to each other's thoughts and sharing our dreams, rather we were doing tasks: running all over Cincinnati picking out patterns for china we would rarely eat on and silverware I've yet to see! Even choosing a cake became a complex task, requiring an investment of hours. Not to mention the dresses and tuxedos, the gifts for groomsmen and bridesmaids, the rehearsal dinner, reservations at the chapel at Miami University where we married, and arrangements for the reception. Whew!

Then we got married and said, "Okay, as soon as we get out of school, we'll have time for each other and we'll work more on our relationship." We didn't.

By then a pattern had developed—a practice of postponement that you too may have experienced. "After grad school we're sure to get more time together," you say to one another, then, "When we get away on vacation this summer, we'll have two weeks just for us." The vacation flies by and soon you're rationalizing again, "When you get settled in your new job, then we'll work on the relationship."

It's not long before children emerge into the picture, and, barely realizing it, this habit of relational postponement is the only way you know to function. From toddler tears to the high school years, there are no real breaks in the parenting schedule. No weeks when the kids turn to you and say, "We'll take care of ourselves this week; why don't you two work on your relationship?" Finally, when the kids leave and the nest is empty, you wake up one morning and look at each other and say, "Who in the heck are you?"

Living Fully Today

In 1938, Thornton Wilder wrote a Pulitzer Prize-winning play called *Our Town*. It's a perennial favorite in high schools. It tells the story of a young woman named Emily who died and is given permission to return to the earth for one memorable day. She can pick any day from her lifetime and relive it moment by moment.

Emily chooses to go back on her twelfth birthday because she remembered it as a happy day. She is soon frustrated, however, at the indifference of those whom she loves. She wishes to engage in life with them but painfully observes that they are just going through the motions, taking each moment totally for granted. As she stands by and watches her birthday take place, she tries to stop it because she can't take it anymore!

She had been reliving her special day, yet no one was experiencing the significant moments. People weren't even looking at each other. Emily cries out, "I can't. I can't go on. It goes so fast. We don't have time to look at one another… Do any human beings ever realize life while they live it?—every, every minute?" [19]

Jesus cautioned about this human tendency. *"Therefore do not worry about tomorrow, for tomorrow will worry about itself. Each day has enough trouble of its own"* (Matt. 6:34). And James 4:14 reiterates: *"What is your life? You are a mist that appears for a little while and then vanishes."* The prophetic implication: live fully today.

If I don't prioritize how and with whom I spend my time, circumstances and other people will decide for me.

Each of us is responsible for our own schedule, how we will order today. If I don't prioritize how and with whom I spend my time, circumstances and other people will decide for me.

My intentional schedule becomes my offering to God. I must prioritize how I will spend my days, how I will create and maintain margins for relationships.

Think about your life today. What relational disciplines do you need in order to make an honorable, excellent offering to God? Relationships provide us with ultimate meaning, but we must create the margins wherein they will flourish.

Mentoring

God's strategy for the transmission of faith and biblical values to future generations is through mentoring-based relationships. It's God's plan for transmitting the DNA of the kingdom of God from person to person, generation to generation.

The transmission is fragile, however, and the handoff has great potential for a fumble. Judges 2:10-11 reminds us: *"After that whole generation had been gathered to their ancestors, another generation grew up who knew neither the LORD nor what he had done for Israel. Then the Israelites did evil in the eyes of the LORD and served the Baals."* The people faithfully served God during Joshua's lifetime, but the next generation did not follow in the values of their parents.

There is a critical difference between ideals and values. Ideals are what you want; values are what you truly live. Your ideals might be that your children grow up and become faithful followers of Jesus, go to college, have fruitful and fulfilling careers, and marry persons of faith, integrity, and intelligence. Values, however, are the realities of their actual choices.

Ideals are what you *want* and values are what you (or your children) actually *do*. Values are demonstrated through our behaviors more than our cognitive beliefs. The challenge is that our values and our beliefs don't always line up: "*For I have the desire to do what is good, but I cannot carry it out. For I do not do the good I want to do, but the evil I do not want to do—this I keep on doing*" (Rom. 7:18-19). How you invest your time, your energy, and your money are the true indicators of your values.

> **How you invest your time, energy, and money are the true indicators of your values.**

Many people in the church have biblical ideals but live secular values. They are functional atheists. In the end, our children will inherit and live out our values, not our ideals.

The People in Your Heart

Our first mentoring responsibility is to the people we have in our heart, our children or those who are emotionally close to home. Psalm 128 reminds us of the priority of the home, and the values that are transmitted therein: "*Your wife will be like a fruitful vine within your house; your children will be like olive shoots around your table*" (Ps. 128:3).

Those closest to us will be adopting our values. When I keep God's practical life disciplines on a daily basis, I will make time priorities for my spouse and children. The women and men who fear the Lord make the mentoring of their family in the values of the kingdom a major priority. This means my family becomes a higher priority than the church where I work.

When Jonathan was in college, Carolyn and I moved to Philadelphia for five weeks to experience his last baseball season at the University of Pennsylvania. From a career perspective this might not have been perceived as a wise decision. The church was in a 20 percent growth climb. It was the Lenten season, leading toward Easter; a busy, important time of year for a pastor! But what is my first "profession"? It's transmitting my kingdom of God values to the next generation.

I had never seen my son hit a college home run. He hit three that year, and I saw all three. Every day I showed up on campus to pitch to Jonathan as part of his practice regimen, much like I had pitched to him in the batting cage at home before he went to college.

Our children follow our values, and our truest values are demonstrated through our time priorities. Parenting is a lifelong intentional time schedule, a career of mentorship. We made a huge investment of our time in Jonathan that spring, and it was a blast. We made memories so precious that Carolyn and I wouldn't trade them for anything.

People need to see leaders who demonstrate the principles of the kingdom of God in their primary relationships.

An amazing side effect of this whole scenario was that the church continued to grow without me. People need to see leaders who demonstrate the priorities of the kingdom of God in their primary relationships.

The opposite effect could have occurred. What a burden we would have put upon Jonathan if he was out there trying to prove himself to us, or get our attention, or struggle to free himself from negative self-talk we had instilled into his life.

A 2002 movie called *The Rookie* is based on the life story of baseball great Jim Morris. Repeated injuries force this aspiring baseball player (played by actor Dennis Quaid) to give up his minor league pitching career and abandon his lifetime ambition to play professional ball. He resorts to the next-best thing: coaching a high school team, which he does in the Texas town where he grew up and his parents still live.

His team, noting their coach's pitching strength during practice, asks why he doesn't try out for the majors again. He responds with a defeatist attitude that mimics his father's distant and non-supportive manner: "I've had my shot," he says, and turns away.

The high-school team, sensing their coach's innate skill,

makes a deal with him: If they win the district championship, he will try out for a major-league ball club. Going from worst to first, the team makes it to state, and their coach is forced to live up to his end of the deal.

Using his amazing fastball, he tries out for and makes the Tampa Bay Devil Rays organization. To top that, he ends up pitching in a major league game as a thirty-five-year-old rookie. At the end of that game, he spots his father, who has by now painfully recognized their relational loss. A conversation ensues, resulting in reconciliation between the two men, a healing moment. "Watching you tonight, not many fathers get a chance to do that," his dad says. "I guess I let too many of those things get away." The dad realized a valuable lesson, that while it is impossible to go back and undo past mistakes, we can still make significant decisions for today.

Whether we're twenty-five or sixty-five, we can choose daily to invest in our key relationships.

Kristen's Perspective

I asked my collaborative writer, Warren Bird, to interview my children. He questioned them about what they felt their priority actually was in Carolyn's and my daily schedule, what values they inherited, and what contradictions they saw between our ideals and those values. They both took the challenge seriously, asking for several days to collect their thoughts.

Kristen, age twenty-six at the time of this writing, says "I always felt my brother and I were top priority with our parents." She remembers them letting her miss school in fifth grade so she could go on a business trip with her dad to San Francisco and Monterey Bay. "They came to all my games at school when I was a cheerleader and on the soccer team," she adds.

She looked forward each year to the annual before-school ritual of her dad taking her to the mall to buy an entire outfit, including shoes and jewelry. "My parents had a way of making me feel special," she says. "They would do anything for me."

The roughest years for Kristen were high school and early college. "My parents were so straight-on," she says. "I felt they were strict and ridiculous. As a teen I'd get very frustrated with them because they put restraints on me and would not budge."

"I gave them a hard time when I was in high school," she acknowledges, but she also remembers her parents' affirmations during those years. "They told my brother and me that we would do more to extend God's kingdom than they ever will."

As an adult, Kristen owns many of her parents' values for herself: "My husband and I share the importance of a relationship with God, of family, of being involved actively in a church community, and of education to better ourselves. My parents taught me that I can do whatever God wants me to do," she affirms.

She says she got her achievement-focus from her dad, but her softer, more emotional side from her mom. "I have high expectations of other people, and that is something I 'caught' from my dad," she says. "But sometimes my parents' high expectations of me clashed with me wanting to be my own person, and it adversely affected our relationship for a few years." The relationship was rebuilt through "prayer on their part and a life-changing decision I made on a mission trip," she explains.

"I'm really thankful for how it turned out," she says. "Had my parents not done all they did—the dad-daughter dates, the special gifts, and investments of time and energy, things they didn't have to do—I don't know how things would have turned out. My parents were real. My mom is my closest friend now," Kristen relays.

Jonathan's Point of View

Jonathan, currently age twenty-three, shares many of Kristen's evaluations. "They put God first, and then family close behind," he says. "They don't just talk about it; they model it. We saw them having devotional time with God in the mornings, they took us to church even when we didn't want to go, and they were always there for our school functions."

"We were a high priority—my Mom gave up her job to raise us kids," Jonathan says. He is quick to identify positive values that he gained from his parents. "From both of them I learned to do things with a 110 percent effort. From Mom, I got my sense of compassion and service, and from Dad I learned how to become a better leader," he says. "'That's not how a leader would act,' my Dad would say, and then he'd coach me on how to do it differently."

Jonathan even sees some of the multi-generational transfers that have taken place. "My dad inherited an intensity from his mother that stays stuck on something until it gets done. That trait developed a perfectionism in me: When I'm a leader, I want it done right first time, and done with excellence—never settling for less than the best."

Sometimes his dad's intensity has led to friction between father and son. "It's hard for Dad to let something drop—something he feels I should or should not do," Jonathan says. Recently Jonathan needed to decide whether to do a second year with Athletes in Action or to take on a different challenge, such as joining Teach for America, which positions promising leaders in under-resourced public schools. "My dad had a strong view," Jonathan says. "Mom had to say, 'Let Jonathan make the decision.'" In the end, Jonathan chose teaching. Jonathan says he trusted God as he worked through that decision, just as his parents had taught him to do.

The intensity-trait works the other way too. "I got my Dad to promise that we'd get matching tattoos," says Jonathan, and he pushed his father for four years until it happened. "I had to take the initiative. It was my ambition more than his, so maybe it got pushed back a bit on my dad's priorities." Both chose to have an ancient Christian symbol tattooed on their right shoulders to make the statement of who and Whose they are.

Occasional raised voices and head butting aside, Jonathan appreciates his parents' style. "Their yes is yes, and no is no," he says. "So when Dad says, 'Trust me on this one,' I often do."

Jonathan saw a model in his parents that he affirms for others. "If you don't put your family just behind God as a priority, and you're not investing in the daily life of your kids, I don't see why adults should get mad if their children aren't close to them when they grow up, or if they don't accept their parent's values. It takes relationship to transfer values between parent and child."

The People in Your Scope

The second mentoring responsibility we have is with the people in our scope—those strategic to God's mission in our network of influence. All people are equally important to God, but all people are not equally strategic to the investment of your time for God's mission. Jesus ministered to the multitudes, but he strategically spent the majority of his time mentoring his twelve disciples. The ultimate test of life success is not measured by what you accomplish or achieve but in who you develop.

Leaders must be strategic with whom they spend their time. As a pastor I learned early on to mark my calendar with strategic think time and strategic people time. It may take two or three weeks for some people to get an appointment to meet with me. I must be a good steward of the time that God has given me, and I must name my own priorities.

You make an impact in the world by making a difference in the lives of other people. It is too easy to become distracted by the wrong priority. Pastors begin to focus on building programs and buildings. Business people pour their energy into building businesses. Teachers turn their attention to lesson plans.

Whatever your type of work, the priority is building people. The ancient Jewish worshipers sang this value as they linked the measure of their work to its influence on people: "*May you see the prosperity of Jerusalem...[and] may you live to see your children's children—peace be on Israel*" (Ps. 128:5-6). My children's children will not know peace unless all of God's children know that same peace. The call of Jesus is a call to make time outside our homes and jobs towards a greater purpose in the world, investing in God's mission through the lives of people.

When I look at where I am and what I've accomplished in life, I envision a circle of people who are standing around me. They are the teachers, coaches, youth mentors, professors, business people, and others who supported Carolyn and me when we made the choice to go into ministry. They are all standing here with words of encouragement, reminding us to be faithful to finish the race well.

Now it's my turn to stand behind someone else, the people in my scope.

Strategic Investments

I set aside time to meet with Mike Berry, a pastor who I am mentoring as the leader of Medway United Methodist Church, a congregation twenty miles east of Ginghamsburg Church. Our bishop was planning to close this aging, dying church, and he asked us if we'd take it under wing and give one last shot at redeveloping it.

God raised up Mike, who had been part of Ginghamsburg. As a civil engineer, Mike had no formal seminary education, but he sensed God's call to invest himself as pastor of this church. What's happening at Medway Church has been nothing short of resurrection—a resurrection that mimics Mike's own conversion.

Fourteen years ago Mike stopped drinking, but a lot of things in his life didn't improve. "I was a recovering alcoholic, and I was taking out my unhappiness on anyone who got in my way, including my dog," he says. His wife, Tracy, had moved out and taken their two children with her. In one final attempt, they decided to try church before the last resort of divorce. "Why don't we see if God will do a miracle?" Tracy suggested.

"We came to church and something happened about ten minutes into the sermon," says Mike. "The Holy Spirit got hold of us, and things have never been the same."

Mike and Tracy rebuilt their marriage around God. "We have grown together, we have grown in ministry, and we have been blessed because of this great God we found at Ginghamsburg Church," Mike says.

It was a seven-year journey between Mike's first visit to Ginghamsburg and what he is doing today as pastor of a United Methodist Church. "My career has been in civil engineering; I can't pastor!" Mike told God when he sensed the initial call. "But through Jesus Christ I can, and I am only getting started in serving the Lord."

Mike has learned most of what he knows by being mentored through Ginghamsburg's example. "They asked me to take food to a needy family," Mike explains. "Then they asked me to pray with the family when I got there. They asked me to lead a Christian twelve-step group, and then to become a care pastor. A couple of years later, they asked me to conduct a funeral. On all of these requests, I said 'I can't.' But with each new experience I learned to tap into God's strength."

Mike meets regularly with me for a "Tuesday at two" mentoring session. He asks me to share experiences and ideas for reaching more people for Jesus Christ. "I usually come with a list of questions about my own walk with the Lord or about how to lead a church more effectively," Mike notes.

Mike started his church appointment in October 2003, with an attendance of seventy to eighty persons. Within eighteen months it was climbing through 150. More remarkably, the age of the average attendee has dropped thirty years, and the church has grown from just a handful of children to fifty during that same period. "The momentum of the church has changed from relatively flat and dead into a mission-driven church," says Mike. "Now ministry is happening every day of the week, from our food pantry to small groups in homes. And I'm still putting family above ministry in my own priorities. My wife and family are located immediately after my personal relationship with Jesus."

"My greatest fulfillment," Mike says, "is that God could use a bottom-feeder like me, someone so off-track in life, to help others become new creatures in Christ, to grow and change." (View Mike Berry's story at www.ginghamsburg.org/mfl.)

I am thankful to be investing in this key relationship.

Identify Your Relational Investments

Who is in the invisible line of people standing behind you? Teachers, coaches, scout leaders, church leaders, campus ministers, professors, or business people? Who has encouraged you, given you a break, or even supported you financially?

I wouldn't be who I am or do what I am doing today if it weren't for these people. Who stands behind you? Who has invested in your life that allows you to stand where you are standing today?

And who are you standing behind? Who are you parenting, mentoring, coaching, encouraging, managing, or leading? Who is receiving the intentional, strategic time in your schedule for relationship building? The investment you are making in people today is the only investment that will live beyond your lifetime, so invest wisely, reminding others to be faithful and finish well.

Momentum for Life Devotional

Read aloud the main Scripture, Psalm 128.

1. Think about the idea that Work + Relationship = Worship. Do you lean more towards work or relationships?

2. Describe the dinner table in the home where you were raised.

3. When was the last crisis that caused you to realize you are not in control? Did you take any positive steps towards the people in your life at that time?

4. Name one person outside your immediate family whose life you are influencing towards God.

5. Share with the group an action step that God is pressing on your heart...something you need to:
   • Say to someone
   • Schedule into your day
   • Do as a relational investment

CHAPTER FIVE
Visioning for the Future

VISION> *The act of seeing or the ability to see; a picture formed in the mind; imaginative foresight; a supernatural apparition.*

"Our feet are standing in your gates, Jerusalem."
(Ps. 122:2)

We live in a world where change is constant. Look at the major innovations that have become part of our everyday lives during the last ten years. We have not only integrated these advancements into our everyday routines but have become so dependent on these emergent technologies for the transaction of our daily affairs that we would be immobilized without them.

• **Internet:** It is amazing how dependent I have become on the Internet—the electronic network that connects computers around the world. It gives me everything from instant information to the world's largest music store. I have two offices, one at home and one at the church, each containing a modest library of books. For the same price as one of those books, I can buy access for a month to a million books. With the Internet, I have access to libraries all over the world. Until recent years, it would have been unheard of for a person in my profession not to have a rather extensive library for the adequate preparation of sermons. Now the Internet provides almost limitless streams of information from everywhere imaginable, all while I sit in my favorite chair. The same thing happens with music. As a teen I would buy 45-rpm records for ninety-nine cents each. Now for the same money I can go, without ever leaving my home, to a digital jukebox called iTunes (www.itunes.com) and download my favorite song. The sound is better quality than those black plastic discs with grooves on them! I also use the Internet to pay bills, order airline tickets, buy specialized motorcycle parts at an online auction, and check my bank balances.

• **Cell phone:** Earlier I described the mission trip where Carolyn and I were teaching at a camp in the mountains of the Czech Republic. We were three hours from a major city, but we could use our cell phone to call our children back in the United States to see how their day was going. We could take pictures on that same phone and e-mail them so our children could see what we were seeing. We also use our cell phones to play video games, log onto the Internet, or receive IM's—instant text messages.

• **E-mail:** I am sending 90 percent less mail through the U.S. postal service and am saving a lot of money on the long-distance telephone calls and phone conferences that I used to make. Many people at Ginghamsburg choose to receive the church's newsletter by e-mail. What an incredible savings on trees, paper and postage! The stewardship that can be applied through the use of this technology makes resources available for the vital mission of Jesus in setting oppressed people free.

• **Portable computers and PDAs (personal digital assistants):** I have come to expect and depend on the ability to have wireless Internet access wherever I am working in my travels. If I'm in a coffee shop, airport, conference facility, hotel, school, library, or church, I get frustrated when a wireless Internet connection is not available. Going wireless gives me a tremendous sense of freedom and a much-increased productivity.

• **Memory storage disks** (CDs and DVDs). The whole idea of recordable, portable disks brings our culture to another place. I can put a dozen translations of the Bible or the news story a local television station did about our inner-city clubhouse ministry—all on one disk.

• **Digital cameras:** I can't remember when I bought my last roll of film! I changed in 2003 from the 35mm format to a digital camera. I love it. I don't have to buy film or wait for it to be developed. I get instant, high-quality results with a reusable, easily portable memory card.

> If my life's work is to be an honorable, excellent offering to God, I can't ever afford to become content or comfortable to stay where I am.

These changes, all in one decade, affirm that we live in a time of exponential-revolutionary change. If my life's work is to be an honorable, excellent offering to God, I can't ever afford to become content or comfortable to stay where I am.

The Power of Vision

The essence of faith is vision. *"Faith is being sure of what we hope for and certain of what we do not see. This is what the ancients were commended for"* (Heb. 11:1-2). These verses come from one of my favorite chapters in the Bible. Hebrews 11 defines the hallmarks of faith, showcasing people of God who are always stretching forward. They long for a better world, a heavenly one, where the peace of God rules for every person. As long as one person lacks the peace and wellness of God, then the love and purpose of God compels the true follower of Jesus forward for the well-being of the planet.

Abraham could not be content with his personal wealth or the rich blessings that he experienced within the comfort his family.

At a ripe old age he left everything that was familiar to make a journey of ascent. *"For he was looking forward to the city with foundations, whose architect and builder is God"* (Heb. 11:10). Faith is looking forward, living with a forward focus. Abraham's task and ours is to work together with God for a better world; that is why we are here.

Until I came into a relationship with Jesus, life was all about me. When Jesus came into my life, I became a partner with him in re-imagining God's purpose for planet Earth. We're working together, building a heavenly planet, a place where the peace of God rules for every person. If one person in the world does not have God's peace, then my call is to start another worship celebration, preach another sermon, build another relationship, or strike up another conversation.

Life isn't meant to get easier with increased age and income. My job is to be on a life-long Psalm of Ascent. With the power of vision, I am always moving forward to become my best *in* the world and *for* the world.

Through the Holy Spirit we have access to the mind of Christ, which enables us to have connection to the limitless ideas of God.

Vision is the natural result of living in the fullness of the Holy Spirit. On the day of Pentecost, the Apostle Peter quotes from the Prophet Joel: *"In the last days, God says, I will pour out my Spirit on all people. Your sons and daughters will prophesy, your young men will see visions, your old men will dream dreams"* (Acts 2:17). Through the Holy Spirit we have access to the mind of Christ, which enables us to have connection to the limitless ideas of God.

This is why I make it a daily practice to intentionally envision God's purpose and direction for my future. Establishing a daily discipline of visioning for God's future is critical. It allows me to formulate a life picture, articulate a healthy-positive life attitude, and initiate strategic life actions.

Formulate a Picture of Life

All physical realities begin with a mental picture. Vision is about formulating, developing, and giving birth to that new reality. God's vision is developed and birthed through real followers of Jesus. Just as God birthed Earth's Savior through the available womb of a servant named Mary, God is still seeking available servants through whom miracles for the salvation of the world can be born. Every new creation begins in the mind of God. *"In the beginning was the Word, and the Word was with God, and the Word was God...The Word became flesh and made his dwelling among us."* (John 1:1,14, NIV) This pattern starts with creation itself. God conceived it, articulated the mental thought, and the Word became material reality.

The architects who designed your office, church, or home didn't start with a bulldozer. Before a shovel was ever put into the ground, they saw something in their minds—a picture in detail. They articulated it through a blueprint that was used for the actual construction. Every single piece in the building was designed by beginning with a picture in a person's mind.

The vision process works the same for you and me. You must be able to conceive an idea before you can achieve it! God wants to birth a miracle through your life's work, but you must be willing to *receive* it by submission to Jesus' authority in your life. You then have to *conceive* the big idea of God through the disciplines of daily Devotion and Readiness for lifelong learning. As you gain skill in the practice of active listening—*"Be still, and know that I am God"* (Ps. 46:10)—God will *achieve* miracles through you.

Visioning is the disciplined practice of formulating God's specific purpose for your life.

The sequence is powerful: receive, conceive, and achieve. It results in visioning—the disciplined practice of formulating God's specific purpose for your life.

Jeremiah was an effective prophet, but before Jeremiah could be used by God, he had to formulate God's vision. The first question God asked Jeremiah was, *"What do you see?"* (Jer. 1:11, 13). All physical realities begin with a mental picture. This is why you have to be careful about what picture is nurtured, which is why pornography, lust, and everything else you allow into your mind truly matters. Your thoughts become the root of your physical fruit.

People tend to live with one of two different perspectives. Some have a microscopic view of life, and others have a telescopic view. Which one is your primary perspective?

If you have a microscopic perspective, your perception of life is based on your current circumstances: what you see, what you feel, and what you hear in the present moment. You are focused on the immediate.

When my bishop moved me to Ginghamsburg Church, I was excited. I knew God was going to shake the world from the little hamlet of Ginghamsburg.

But the first time my mother came and saw our two-room country church building with fewer than one hundred people and a $27,000 annual budget, she felt and saw something very different. To her, the only thing here was a church in a terrible location with limited facilities and full of people who were resistant to growth and change. "My, my, my. What have they done to my baby? You have a Master's degree!" she bemoaned.

A person with a microscopic view tends to focus on life's problems. They center on obstacles and limitations. Microscopic people often approach life with a scarcity mentality.

Some of Jesus' disciples did that. When he presented them with the challenge of feeding 5,000 people, all they could see were problems, obstacles, and limitations. "Where are we going to get the money?" "There are too many people." "The closest food is more than an hour away." (see John 6:5-7.)

In contrast, the person with a telescopic perspective is looking forward to what God is creating in the future. While microscopic people focus on the problem, telescopic people see the possibilities. They have confidence that *"all things are possible with God"* (Mark 10:27).

The prophet Elisha had a possibility focus. He had become a thorn in the side of the king of Aram, who was seeking to destroy Israel. The king of Aram would say, "Set an ambush here," but Elisha would send a message to the king of Israel: "Watch out when you're passing this place, because Aram has set an ambush there." This kind of thing happened frequently, and the king of Aram became furious at Elisha.

The king of Aram sent out spies to discover Elisha's whereabouts. They learned that he was in a city called Dothan, or perhaps on its outskirts, so the king dispatched an impressive fighting force of horses and chariots. They came by night and surrounded the city.

Upon awakening in the morning, Elisha's servant made the grim discovery of the imminent danger. Needless to say, he had a microscopic response and was ready to run up the white flag immediately. *"Oh no, my lord! What shall we do?"* (2 Kings 6:15), he asked in a panic.

Elisha on the other hand was not looking with the eyes of his head. He was seeing through the eyes of his heart, looking forward to what God was creating in the future. *"Don't be afraid. Those who are with us are more than those who are with them"* (v. 16). What on earth was Elisha talking about? There was a sum total of two: Elisha and his servant. *"And Elisha prayed, 'Open his eyes, LORD, so that he may see.' Then the LORD opened the servant's eyes, and he looked and saw the hills full of horses and chariots of fire all around Elisha"* (v. 17).

The servant saw the urgency of the immediate crisis, and Elisha saw the armies of heaven.

I am a telescopic person. I didn't see a little country church building. I saw something bigger in impact than what I even yet see today. I am always looking forward to what God is creating in the future.

Vision—a promising picture of God's preferred future—gives energy to initiate and sustain the journey of ascent.

If I am not taking time every day to envision a better reality, I will reach my picture and retire. I can't conceive of retirement because I am constantly, every day, formulating a picture of what God is creating in the future. In fact my picture is so big that I have started to worry, "I am fifty-three; how am I going to get this done by the time I die?"

Vision can be defined as a promising picture of God's preferred future. It creates greater energy and generates bigger strategic actions. It gives energy to initiate and sustain the journey of ascent.

Envision a Destination

Vision is focused on the promised destination. Many parents have a common experience when taking their young children on a vacation or outing in the car. Carolyn and I would be heading to Florida on spring break. We couldn't reach the Ohio state line before our kids would say, "When are we going to get there?" and "Are we there yet?" Most parents have heard that question a zillion times.

I remember the "are we there yet?" experience of my childhood family's first long vacation. It was 1958, and I was seven years old. My dad had just bought a brand new blue and white Chevy Belair. We were going 1,300 miles to my uncle's house on Key Biscayne Island near Miami. This was before the interstate highway system was up, so it took us three long days. With no air conditioning and plastic covers on the seats, my hairline hurt from the wind blowing through our open windows.

What sustained me was my uncle's description of the ocean. Before we left, he was talking to me on the telephone, telling me about the ocean and beach. I had never seen the ocean. Uncle Doc's picture of the promised destination—his description of the beach—sustained me for the three-and-a-half day journey.

It was no doubt tempting for my parents, in light of the incessant complaints coming from my sister and me in the back seat, to stop short of their destination. Our second night was in the beautiful hills of Tennessee, a great spot for a vacation. But they had made a focused commitment to arrive at my uncle's house in Key Biscayne.

One of the early Psalms of Ascent, sung toward the beginning of the journey to Mt. Zion, contained a visual reminder of the destination. The people's intention was to "*go to the house of the* LORD" (Ps. 122:1). What was the picture these Israelite worshipers held in their heads? "*Our feet are standing in your gates Jerusalem*" (v. 2). They held onto that picture, a vision of their destination, until they got there. That is similar to the formation of your own life's blueprint for the realization of God's future in your life.

When I came to a small, semi-rural country church, I didn't picture myself as a pastor of a little church with ninety people and a $27,000 annual budget in a two-room facility on less than an acre of land. I envisioned myself as the pastor of thousands. I acted, thought, and planned as the leader of thousands. That was the picture I believed was from God.

A Growing Vision

Visioning is a daily process of formulating and refining my own life calling. After one of my times of <u>D</u>evotion in 2005, I spent over a half hour reading about the current crisis in the Sudan. My reading ties into the discipline of <u>R</u>eadiness for lifelong learning. I've been following the plight of Sudan, where a lack of food, the spread of disease, and the ongoing conflict has torn apart the lives of more than three million people, mostly children and women. The U.S. Congress has labeled the situation in Sudan as genocide. World attention is at last looking into the reports of government-backed militias, mass murder, systematic sexual violence, and brutal slaughter of Christians. It's being called the world's worst humanitarian crisis.

In late 1998, when the biggest known problem in Sudan was starvation from massive crop failure, God began to give me a picture of what we could do. Citing Isaiah 58, I reminded the congregation, "You have power with God by your actions toward people, especially people in need." In 1999, I held up a *Dayton Daily News* photo of Sudan next to a

Why are we well-educated in the sedan but oblivious to starvation in the *Sudan*?

photo ad on the same section of the paper for a new BMW. Then I said, "It says 770,000 people are on the verge of death because of starvation, and I didn't even know about it. I'm very aware of the BMW sedans, including the twelve-speaker sound system and the sixteen-position reclining seats. What bothers me is that I'm far less aware of the Sudan." Why are we well-educated in the *sedan* but oblivious to starvation in the *Sudan?*

We took action, beginning to give generously and sacrificially, wanting to live out the heart of God and compassion of Jesus. "People are dying, and we're oblivious," I reminded our congregation. We began to wake up from our selfishness. Most recently, Ginghamsburg middle-school students alone raised $4,000 to build two fresh-water wells. A congregation-wide offering on Christmas 2004 sent $312,000 to the United Methodist Committee on Relief, funding an agricultural-development program that is assisting more than 250 Sudanese families.

By Lent 2005, my vision was spreading to others, namely a cell group of servants in the church who were available for God's vision to be birthed through them as well. These men and women conceived, articulated, and ultimately achieved an additional offering for hunger relief. The idea was for each person in our church to fast one meal a week and put the cost of that meal into an envelope. The offerings would be collected as a special Easter offering we held at Ginghamsburg, and given toward Sudanese hunger relief. They called it Fast for Famine. (View the story about Fast for Famine and the Sudan Miracle Offering at www.ginghamsburg.org/mfl.)

That's why I keep praying, reading, and learning about the Sudan. As I reflected on that recent morning, I paused to spend a half hour running (see the next chapter on Eating and Exercise). Then Carolyn and I had breakfast together. Over breakfast I began to draw a picture for her of the orphanage that I picture our church constructing in 2006 for the children in the Sudan. I saw the picture complete with a guesthouse so that we can have medical and support teams on the premises twelve months out of the year. Elsewhere there would be dormitories, classrooms, and a chapel. We will then raise scholarships for each of the children who live in the orphanage to attend African University, which is a United Methodist school.

My sketch was not a sudden, hastily assembled plan. It represents a vision that grows and is refined every day. It's a blueprint for the realization of God's picture. I take time every day to visualize God's promised future. I know that if my vision is fuzzy or clouded, this will affect everyone I influence and am connected to. How great the cost would be if I allowed God's vision to be interrupted and ultimately omitted from the lives of those in my circle of care. Leaders must faithfully receive, conceive, and work to achieve the picture of God's promised destination.

Vision is a contagious commodity, by the way. It can captivate a church of any size. The pastor of a church of one hundred people came to one of our conferences and was inspired by what we were doing in the Sudan. He went back and led his church to make miracle offering of over $7,000 for the Sudan.

Another person, from a church of 200, went home from a different Ginghamsburg conference convicted of her personal need to be financially free so that she could better respond to others in need. "One theme kept jumping out at me, which at first I tried in vain to ignore and suppress," she wrote us. "It was the issue of financial health—tithing and being debt-free…As you talked about our responsibility as Christians not to allow mediocrity in any area of our lives, I came to tears as I felt God right beside me, encouraging me to let go of this one area of my life in which I'd not yet allowed Him to be Master and to trust Him with my whole life…In my heart I yielded completely to God and promised to act immediately to bring true health to my financial situation." She then drove back to her hometown. Even before she went to her house, she met with a friend from church who helped her take steps to bring her financial situation under control.

As John Wesley repeatedly told his followers, "Catch on fire for God and people will come and watch you burn!" Vision pulls us upward to bolder life actions. When you and I are dreaming God-size dreams, we don't have the time to contemplate retirement. I figure I

Vision pulls us upward to bolder life actions.

need to live to age 127 to accomplish all the plans that God is igniting in my heart. People retire because they get tired of doing the same old things. God creates new wine that makes our life's work and creations new every morning!

Persevering Towards the Future

Vision also inspires perseverance. After Moses' death, Joshua accepted the call and challenge to lead God's people into the land of promise. *"I will give you every place where you set your foot, as I promised Moses"* (Josh. 1:3). After making this promise to Joshua, God then provided a more detailed blueprint for a vast expanse of territory that extends from the Euphrates River in the east to the Mediterranean Sea in the west (see Josh. 1:4).

God's promise is a done deal. All Joshua and the people of God have to do is keep on stepping forward. The verses that follow exhort Joshua, in effect, "Don't stop, look back or deviate to the left or the right. In the face of opposition and conflict, just keep on keeping on. Stay on the journey of ascent. Don't become comfortable or satisfied when you begin to be filled with fruits that are produced in the land of milk and honey. The abundance that you experience today is not yet the place of ultimate promise. The resistance that you meet tomorrow is not the place of ultimate defeat. Don't quit, stop, or settle for anything less than the realization of the place of promised destination that you visualized when you first heard God call your name."

A good friend who has been closely acquainted with my ministry regularly reminds me of my ordinary-ness. "Mike, if I look at any one of your twenty-five years here—no matter which one I pick—I can't point to any one year that you've done anything really great...the thing is, you just don't go away!"

My friend is right. I just keep walking towards the vision God gave me when I came here in April, 1979. At that time I was very concerned with discovering God's mission for the church. I knew that this little country church had been in existence since 1863. I also knew that each of the people involved would have an opinion of his or her own. At twenty-seven years of age, I sensed that my life and ministry were too short to be about anything less than the purpose of God. So I established, as my first priority, the ability to "see" God's purpose.

As I tell the story in my first book, *Spiritual Entrepreneurs:* "On a chilly but sunny April morning, I went and stood in a field behind the little two-room church building—the site of our current counseling center. Staring back at the modest church facility that looked like hundreds of others, I said: 'Lord, I am not going to leave this field until I have a clear sense of your mission for this church.'

"...I remained in the field for the rest of the afternoon. And as is so often the case, God speaks, not through storm, fire, or earthquake, but through silence. God's thoughts began to stream into my head. I could see three thousand people worshiping the Lord. A deep sense of God's feeling for the lost overwhelmed me. I am not a highly emotional person, but tears ran down my cheeks as I sensed God's pain for the people who lived thirty minutes in every direction from this location—people who had no understanding of God's love and healing intention.

"...I had a vision of a church that would be a teaching church, a place where ordinary people would come and be equipped to be fully assimilated and functioning members of the Body of Christ—disciples who would go out into the marketplace and win the lost; followers of Jesus who would be committed to work in the inner city in ministries to help set free the oppressed; people of compassion who would do lay counseling and develop support-group ministries. A picture of pastors and lay people coming to this place from other churches was forming in my spirit. They would come here to see what God was doing and take what they learned back to other churches, throughout our denomination and beyond, promoting renewal."

I also saw a church that represented ethnic diversity, where the songs of all cultures were sung and celebrated.

"When I left the field it was late afternoon. I left with a sunburn and a clear sense of God's purpose, which has kept me moving forward and sustained me during my ministry at Ginghamsburg Church. This experience has been the basis for everything that has taken place. The power of vision enabled me to see the reality of God's success before it happened.

"When a leader has a clear picture of God's destination, the people begin to articulate and live that vision. Over a period of time, that vision begins to penetrate the surrounding culture...Vision clarifies God's purpose and direction."[20]

Too many pastors and other leaders leave their church or place of employment in the face of resistance and opposition. They never experience the promise of God because they quit stepping forward; they start over again back at the beginning.

You will never reach God's place of promise if you keep starting over. Many people not only do this in their life's work but also in their relationships. I was headed that way when I nearly gave up on my marriage to Carolyn. We were at the twenty-year mark in our frustration of pain and failure. I am so thankful that we didn't make our decision on the basis of what we were seeing, feeling, and hearing at that present moment. We chose instead to focus on what God was intending and creating for our relationship in the future. We began to build daily on the promising picture of God's preferred future. As of this writing we are celebrating more than thirty years of marriage and are allowing God to use our lives as a source of health and blessing for others.

Nurtured in Community

Vision is nurtured in community. The Psalms of Ascent were sung in community.

You cannot climb the incline of faith by yourself. As you and I travel together on this journey, we hear each other's words and stories of faith.

Steve is a physician in our church who leads medical mission teams several times a year to locations all over the world. After a recent trip he was sharing with me how $40,000 a year would support an orphanage of 300 children in a third-world country. My vision was triggered. I began to dream about how we as a local church could build and support schools and orphanages all around the world. What if we could get all the United Methodist churches in my *annual conference* to support this project? What if we could get every United Methodist in the *state* to give the equal amount of the total that they spend on Christmas toward world hunger and oppression? What if every Christian in the *country* would...? What if every Christian in the *world* would...? The vision began to stir because I heard Steve's song of ascent as we were together.

We cannot make this journey alone. We cannot carry ourselves to the place of wholeness or to the fulfillment of our intended destinies.

I admire the story in Mark 2:1-11 where the four men carry their paralyzed friend to Jesus. They were faithful, persistent, innovative, and resourceful. That's a rather creative group! Think about the energy it would take to get this one person, dead weight, up onto a roof and then to cut through the roof to get him down again, into the healer's care.

Notice that it took four people to bring this man to Jesus. Have you discovered that you can't get there by yourself? I appreciate this saying, "No one goes to heaven by themselves; we go in groups." Like the paralyzed man, you need someone to carry you. Carolyn and I would have never made it without others around us to bring us to healing in our relationship, nor would I have stayed at Ginghamsburg without others to help me along.

Some people come to church and say to themselves, "I can hang out by myself, come here, be inspired every weekend, and that's good enough." It's not. You need help to find Jesus through the crowd. You need the faith of your friends when your own faith falters. The paralyzed man was healed, *"when Jesus saw their faith"* (v. 5). Whose faith did Jesus see? The faith of the man's friends.

Sometimes I want to ask, "God, where are you?" Do you ever feel that way? I've even found myself occasionally saying, "Is this Jesus thing for real?" We have more faith together than we do alone by ourselves; sometimes when it's too hard for me to trust God, other people can trust for me.

We have more faith together than we do alone by ourselves.

Leland, a ninety-four-year-old friend of mine, helps lower friends through rooftops to be touched by Jesus. "If I sit down at the donut shop and I don't know the person next to me, I strike up a

conversation," Leland says. "Where do you go to church?" he asks them. If they say they don't go anywhere, Leland takes it as his signal to go after them. "I would say eighteen to twenty have been fetched in by my invitation," Leland reports. He doesn't just invite. He picks them up in his car and brings them to church. "At ninety-four, I won't be around here much longer," he explains, "So I want to cover as much territory in this spiritual aspect as I can. We're told that one of the things we are to do is to be about Jesus' business. So as long as I'm able, I'll be contacting individuals about their spiritual status." (View Leland's story at www.ginghamsburg.org/mfl.)

People like Leland get involved. They're resourceful. Since the men could not get their paralyzed friend to Jesus through normal means, they made an opening in the roof above Jesus. In other words, they made doors where there were no doors. After they carved through the roof, can you imagine the mess? I can hear the synagogue people below: "We just put the roof on this building last year!" Jesus didn't die for shingles and nails; he died for paralyzed people who depend on the vision of others to bring them into the community of care and transformation.

Who are your traveling companions? Are you being pulled forward by the collective vision of those in your faith community? Each of us is responsible for developing our own network of mentoring relationships. Vision is nurtured in community, prophetic communities that bring people to Jesus, who then grow in authentic relationships and become empowered to serve.

Articulate a Healthy-Positive Life Attitude

The tongue is a powerful force that has the potential to bring life or death. "*A word out of your mouth may seem of no account, but it can accomplish nearly anything—or destroy it!*" (James 3:5, The Message). Our words create the physical realities of our attitudes. The songs that we sing in the rigors of the journey are songs of celebration, faith, and victory. "*If the Lord had not been on our side…the flood would have engulfed us, the torrent would have swept over us, the raging waters would have swept us away. Praise be to the Lord"* (Ps. 124:1, 4-6).

Vision empowers me to sing songs of faith in the face of discouragement and resistance. When you grasp God's vision for your life's work, you celebrate what is right with life. You focus on the positive, redemptive activity of God that is going on continually all around us. When you celebrate the good, you build vision for God's possibilities and you find energy to fix what's wrong!

We speak faith and hope on the basis of God's promise and not out of the circumstances of the moment. Faith is demonstrated in the action of trust. When Peter, crossing the Sea of Galilee in a terrifying storm, heard the voice of Jesus that seemed to come from an uncertain apparition on the water, he took an irrational risk and stepped out of the boat to attempt the impossible. *"'Lord, if it's you,' Peter replied, 'tell me to come to you on the water'"* (Matt. 14:28).

Trust is fortified through our verbal attitudes. The ancient Jewish pilgrims affirmed that they would trust God regardless of their current circumstances. *"Those who trust in the LORD are like Mount Zion, which cannot be shaken but endures forever"* (Ps. 125:1). Regardless of how the earth moves, vision allows them to have positive, healthy attitudes. *"Our mouths were filled with laughter, our tongues with songs of joy"* (Ps. 126:2).

We are trusting God's promise. We are not heading toward defeat but toward victory, surplus, and abundance. One person said to me, "Mike, what we are doing in the Sudan is like throwing our resources down an empty pit." I couldn't disagree more. God is preparing a banquet for the life of the world. He takes the meager offering of stale bread and few fish and multiplies abundantly that all might eat and be satisfied.

The Lord is *"on our side,"* affirms Psalm 124:1. Looking ahead to the back of the book, God wins in the end. Jesus died on the cross and resurrected from the grave, and the victory is final. Jesus' salvation is offered to every single person on planet Earth. I might not see the realization of it today, but as long as I am going to die anyway, I am going to sow my life toward God's future.

People of vision are determined to articulate a healthy-positive life attitude in all they do. When I came to this little country church, I kept telling stories of what God was going to do in the future. I didn't focus on the inadequate building, the backwoods location, the meager resources, or the resistance to growth and change. Jesus did not die so that God's mission would fail. And so I keep speaking the promising picture of God's preferred future in spite of the negativity or resistance that I might be experiencing in the heat of the moment. As the pilgrims long ago sang in their Psalm of Ascent, *"They have greatly oppressed me from my youth, but they have not gained the victory over me"* (Ps. 129:2).

People of vision are determined to articulate a healthy-positive life attitude in all they do.

Initiate Strategic Actions

Vision empowers leaders to initiate strategic actions that result in a picture of life. Walt Kallestad and Kirbyjon Caldwell, in their book, *Entrepreneurial Faith*, name a leading cause of plateau among leaders. "One of the main causes of burnout among pastors and other leaders is that they don't execute their visions. They spend all their time and energy dancing around worn-out systems—sacred cows—and never see their vision fulfilled. After awhile, they simply give up."[21]

God entrusts vision to those who will faithfully execute the vision! The size of vision that God gives is dependent on our faithfulness to implement strategic action.

Ginghamsburg's approach to Fast for Famine started in a cell group in our church. They had participated in the Ginghamsburg Christmas offering for Sudan, and they wanted to do something that would keep the momentum going all year long. They couldn't shake the idea that 800 million people around the world go hungry each day. They calculated that everyone who voted in the last presidential election gave up one meal, it would equate to $400 million.

"I was sitting down one day, thinking about what we could do and what a shame it is that so many people are without even one basic meal a day," says Ron, initial creator of the idea. "All of a sudden this voice came into my head and said, 'I want *you* to do it.' I replied out loud, 'What?' But as I began to see each individual person plugging in at different levels, I immediately saw a part that I could play." This small group has developed a Web site (www.fastforfamine.org) and has a vision of raising $100 million in the coming years.

There are enough resources today to feed the world, and America, the world's largest food exporter, could take the lead.[22] So why can't we do something so that the people of Sudan can grow enough food? Why can't we do something to help hungry people here at home? God wants to do incredible things, but he will not give you a vision that exceeds the size of the faith-steps that you are willing to take.

God is looking for people who will faithfully act on whatever ideas he places in their mind, in spite of their fear or reservations.

God has given us everything we need according to his riches in Christ Jesus our Lord. Vision empowers us to initiate life-changing action. God will not trust us with a bigger vision than we are willing to implement. God wants to accomplish much on planet Earth, but he is looking for people who will faithfully act on whatever ideas he places in their mind, in spite of their fear or reservations.

God gives big visions to people who are willing to take big actions! Leadership is not about doing the expected things that others around you have experienced from managers of sacred traditions that have preceded you. Leadership implements the risky strategic actions necessary to reach God's place of promise. Leaders are driven by dreams and visions and not by the expectations or reprisals of people. They are compelled forward by truth, not motivated by the accolades of committees. Leaders do the right thing rather than the expected thing.

A Strategic Action Plan

Every year I work from a strategic action plan. I get confused by all the business models that present the need for vision statements, mission statements, purpose statements, and highly detailed plans. For me it's simple. I get a clear vision, and I spell out the strategic actions that I will implement this year to get closer to God's place of promise.

This is far more important than a wish list. It is not just an idea ("I'd like to do something big for God"), and it is more than a strategic goal ("I'll need to look into beginning a new worship celebration sometime soon"). It does no good if it is never executed. That is why I work from a yearly strategic action plan. For example, my one-year strategic plan for 2005 had a three-prong focus: to start a Saturday evening worship celebration for people in recovery, by Easter; to define and implement phase two of our Sudan initiative, by October; and to assure the inception of one hundred new cell groups by December 31st. I continue to work and plan as if I have one year to live. I call it my one-year rule. This approach allows me to prioritize on the basis of mission-critical-strategic activities. More importantly it gives me permission not to do things of less importance.

Two years ago our church was gearing up to start planning a new, $10 million sanctuary that would seat 3,000. Then I asked myself the question, "If I had just one year to live, would I spend it building a worship center?" My conclusion felt right: "I don't want to spend this precious time building facilities; I want to build people." Current research is telling us that the postmodern generation doesn't relate to the mega-mall worship structures that are built by the boomer generation. They prefer smaller, more intimate venues. My new slogan became, "Minimize brick, maximize mission."

That same one-year strategic focus helped Carolyn and me in our decision to move to Philadelphia for Jonathan's senior year baseball season. It was named as a personal strategic action plan.

There are four areas to consider in a yearly strategic action plan:

1. Self-Health. If I am not healthy spiritually, emotionally, and physically, then I can't be a source of health and hope to those around me. I plan self-health activities into my daily schedule.

2. Relationships. We are created for relationships, and relationships are created in the margins of our lives. I strategically make my family a priority as I plan my strategic direction for each week, month, and year.

3. Work. Our work is not separate from our relationship with God. Our work is an act of worship. If my work is to continue on the upward ascent of being an honorable, excellent offering to God, then I need to be growing in my daily execution. I regularly ask myself: What am I doing this year that is different than what I did last year? What new worship experiences, programs, groups, or missions have been initiated? What people have been identified as potential new leaders? It is terribly easy to get stuck in the rut of doing things in the same old ways and to keep recycling the same tired, stagnant, or burned-out workers. If God is always wanting to do a new thing, we can't put new wine in old wineskins.

4. Mission. God holds each of us accountable for a personal mission outside of our families and workplace. A church's mission is driven by multitudes of unpaid men and women who are faithfully carrying out Christ's mission to win the lost and set the oppressed free. Scouting programs, youth sports, Christian education, camp counselors, food pantries, homeless shelters, and tutoring programs cannot function apart from commitment to sacrificial service.

I am currently working with a group of young college and postgraduate students to help them become the radical, excellent Christian leaders of their generation. We meet periodically in different parts of the country for leadership-learning experiences. I assign them regular reading, and I am raising a young hero scholarship fund for any of these young people who pursue graduate work for the purpose of vocational ministry. This personal mission strategy is separate from my home or work commitments.

The K.I.S.S. Principle: Keep It Simple Saints

A great strategic plan will focus on a few well-defined and articulated initiatives. Most people try to do too many things in any one given year. What was my one-year strategic action plan for my first year at Ginghamsburg Church? I did three specific things.

First, I preached a sermon series from the book of Acts. This was offered to illustrate the true purpose and mission of the church. As Rick Warren says in the first sentence of *The Purpose Driven Life*, "It's not about you."[23] We are here to serve the mission of Christ. Confusion exists in the church. Our members perceive themselves to be customers when they are to be missionaries! Every week during my first year at Ginghamsburg, I came with a hard-hitting, relevant message from the book of Acts. I challenged each person's worldview by contrasting it with the worldview of Jesus.

Second, I simplified the administrative structure to serve Christ's mission rather than the mission of serving an antiquated structure. The little country church that I had come to had nine boards and committees. The people were spending an average of sixteen nights a month in generally fruitless meetings that really had nothing to do with the true mission of Christ.

People are seeking a life mission, not a meeting!

We now have one board of nine people who meet together one night a month, ten or eleven times a year. Isn't it amazing that one "committee" can lead a church with almost 5,000 in attendance each week, working in mission around the world. Yet the little church I started with had less than one hundred people but nine committees.

People are energized for the mission of Jesus when they have an opportunity to experience significance on the front lines. People are seeking a life mission, not a meeting!

Third, I poured myself into ten strategic leaders who would become the leaders of the movement. In my first three months at

Ginghamsburg church, I identified a small group of influential people who had both heart and skill strengths. Even then I realized that all people are equally important to God, but all people are not equally strategic for the investment of my time toward God's mission.

We met in our home one night a week and practiced the ancient art of discipleship. We read Christian classics like Dietrich Bonhoeffer's *The Cost of Discipleship*. Within months these people went out and started disciple cell groups of their own and became innovative, risk-taking members of our church board. Any organization will stagnate or fail if it has people in decision-making places who are not faithfully envisioning the promised place of the future.

My life—and yours—is too short to live for anything less than a fulfilling, fruitful, faithful purpose. Take time every day to dream God's dream for your life. God gives great vision to those who are willing to take great action!

Momentum for Life Devotional

Read aloud the main Scripture, Psalm 122.

1. Were you raised to be a microscopic person or a telescopic person?

2. Who is/are the person(s) that help(s) nurture your vision?

3. Celebrating what's right gives us energy to fix what's wrong. Do you naturally "speak faith" or feel compelled to say what's wrong in life situations?

4. What life-picture is God showing you that you would like to begin putting into action?

5. Do you know the strategic action steps you must take, or do you need to connect with a strategic partner to help design a plan? What is your next step?

CHAPTER SIX

Eating and Exercise for Life

EAT> *To consume as sustenance; to include something as a usual or fundamental part of a diet.*

EXERCISE> *Activity requiring physical or mental exertion, especially when performed to develop or maintain physical fitness.*

"May the LORD bless you from Zion; may you see the prosperity of Jerusalem all the days of your life. May you live to see your children's children—peace be on Israel." (Ps. 128:5-6)

Have you ever heard someone make a statement like, "I can't wait to go to heaven," or, "I hope that Jesus is coming back soon." I can wait! I am in no hurry to make the celestial trip. It's not that I won't be happy to see Jesus. I'm just really enjoying this incredible gift of life.

Sometimes we have the tendency to be like the spoiled child at Christmas who eagerly rips through the wrappings in the morning but by late afternoon is bored with the gift and discards it. Life is a gift to be embraced and celebrated to the max. I love life's complexities as well as its intricacies. I look forward to my first cup of coffee each morning. I look forward each fall to the first snow. In fact, each of the four seasons continues to bring me a new sense of wonder.

Even the simple day-to-day routines of life add sparkle to my world. I find a richness in pitching baseballs to my son or hearing the enthusiasm in my daughter's voice when she calls on the phone and says, "Hi dad, how are you doing?"

I love marriage, work, food, family, meeting new people, and the experience of traveling the world. I love life, and I am in no hurry to let go of this precious gift.

The Gift of Life

What makes life unique? The breath of God. *"Then the LORD God formed a man from the dust of the ground and breathed into his nostrils the breath of life, and the man became a living being"* (Gen. 2:7). The Hebrew name for Adam sounds like the Hebrew name for dirt. All the elements in a human body can be found in dirt, but you are more than the sum total of chemicals and minerals found in the natural world or molecules charted on the periodic table. God breathed Spirit into the human form, adding a sense of mystery to the essence of human life.

What makes life unique? The breath of God...That's why every human being matters to God.

That's why every human being matters to God. There are no disposable people. That's why Ginghamsburg Church is involved with the Sudan crisis, as millions face the threat of starvation: every single life matters! That's why I personally struggle with the issues of abortion, euthanasia, capital punishment, and war. Every human contains the breath of God that brings life. In God's eyes, every single life has value.

I heard former *Superman* actor Christopher Reeve lecture in Philadelphia in the spring of 2004, just a few months before his death. He couldn't even move his head, totally dependent on a respirator to deliver his breath. His assistant rolled him onto the stage in an elaborate wheelchair. He continued to maximize his gift of life in spite of the overwhelming daily issues of his physical limitations and life-threatening abnormalities.

This is in stark contrast to the Clint Eastwood movie, *Million Dollar Baby*, which won critical acclaim both at the box office and the 2005 Academy Awards. Eastwood's character turned to the solution of euthanasia when the boxer (played by Hilary Swank) experienced the same paralyzing injury as Reeve had in real life. Christopher Reeve demonstrated that the quality and value of life is not tied to the absence of debilitating injuries or disease. His life gave me fresh appreciation for the breath of God.

As a follower of Jesus Christ, no matter what your ability or disability, your body is the dwelling place of God! "*Do you not know that your bodies are temples of the Holy Spirit, who is in you, whom you have received from God? You are not your own; you were bought with a price. Therefore honor God with your bodies*" (1 Cor. 6:19-20).

It is tempting for us to disassociate the selection of foods or the decision to exercise from our commitments to God, but our bodies are no longer our own. We have been purchased, body-mind-spirit, with the redemptive work of God through Jesus' life, death, and resurrection. Eating healthy and making a disciplined commitment to exercise is not an option for the committed follower of Jesus. It is one of the essential daily life *disciplines* of discipleship.

"*Therefore, I urge you, brothers and sisters, in view of God's mercy, to offer your bodies as a living sacrifice, holy and pleasing to God—this is true worship*" (Rom. 12:1). "*Let us purify ourselves from everything that contaminates body and spirit, perfecting holiness out of reverence for God*" (2 Cor. 7:1).

Eating healthy and making a disciplined commitment to exercise is not an option for the committed follower of Jesus.

I am amazed how it is almost impossible to find anything in popular Christian literature about the disciplines associated with eating and exercise. I do find material on fasting from time to time, but it is rarely linked to the purpose of physical health. Yet starting with God's instruction to the Israelites, the Bible has much to say about diet. The Bible is filled with references to the purity of the body in ways that extend beyond our sexual morality. The sin of gluttony—habitual eating to excess—seems to be the acceptable sin for much of the church, clergy, and laity alike. Yet all references to gluttony in the Bible are negative.

We were bought with a price: the life and death of Jesus on the cross. God owns our bodies, so we must honor God in the care of our bodies. Otherwise we cannot continue God's work in the excellence of ascent. God intends to use my physical body through which the Holy Spirit can operate. If God is going to feed dying children in the Sudan, he needs the longevity of my life and assets! The Church is the hands, feet, and mouth of Jesus on planet Earth for reaching the lost and setting oppressed people free. God needs our bodies to complete the mission of Jesus in the world.

Salvation is a lifestyle of (w)holiness. The purpose of Jesus coming into our lives is not only to save us for heaven but to heal us

Salvation is a lifestyle of (w)holiness.

and make us well in every dimension of life, so that our bodies can be honorable, excellent offerings to God. As excellent offerings, our longevity has value for Jesus' mission.

In the past, I've needed to borrow someone else's larger vehicle to get my kids back and forth to college. I've noticed that when I borrow someone else's car I tend to be more careful. There is almost a holy uneasiness in me because it takes us several days back and forth to the East Coast to move our children. In my car, if I spill a little coffee it might get cleaned up next year, but not in someone else's car! The same principle applies to clutter that accumulates on the floor of my car. When I borrow someone else's car, I might have it for two days, but I take the floor mats out and brush them off because I am more careful with someone else's property than I am with my own. I have a different kind of respect.

This respect is similar to what the Bible is saying about our bodies. Our bodies are for the Lord, and we can no longer be indifferent about our physical condition.

The Value of Longevity

The Psalms of Ascent place value on longevity. "*May the LORD bless you from Zion; may you see the prosperity of Jerusalem all the days of your life. May you live to see your children's children—peace be on Israel"* (Ps. 128:5-6).

Your life is a gift from God. You live to serve God's purpose. Health best serves God's mission for the fruitful completion of your life purpose as well as the enjoyment of experiencing the fruits of your life's labors. Why are our fifties, sixties, and seventies called our prime-time years? When you are healthy, you can still enjoy the energy of youthfulness, the wisdom of age, and the fruit of your accumulated years of labor.

Your time of death is not predetermined. It is affected by your life practices and choices. Somehow we don't believe that, or we wouldn't hear so many dumb statements at funerals. "I guess it was just their time to go." Come on! The person who died sped the process by smoking three packs of cigarettes a day and being seventy pounds overweight!

There is evidence from new research suggesting that long life is the result of disciplined life choices. *Time Magazine's* cover article, "How to Live to Be 100," says that the dominant factor is our lifestyle more than our genetic makeup. "You could have Mercedes-Benz genes," says Dr. Bradley Willcox, of the Pacific Health Research Institute in Honolulu, "but if you never change the oil, you are not going to last as long as a Ford Escort that you take good care of."[24] The article cites studies showing that Seventh-day Adventists, who avoid alcohol, caffeine, and tobacco, tend to live an average eight years longer than other Americans.[25] There is no question that a change in eating habits and physical exercise can prolong our lives through greater health and vitality into our seventies, eighties, and beyond.

Achieving maximum length and quality of life requires hard work and discipline. Obesity is one of the leading causes of preventable death in the United States. Being extremely overweight is indisputably lethal, according to the Centers for Disease Control and Prevention.[26] From 1991 to 2000, the percentage of obese Americans increased by 61 percent.[27]

Diet programs abound, but do people stay with them long enough to see lasting benefit? From Atkins to South Beach, Americans are forking over millions in hopes of finding a magic elixir while we continue to pack on the pounds. One calculation says that a third of Americans are not just overweight but obese.[28]

Obesity is also reaching epidemic proportions among our children! It tripled among seven- to fifteen-year-olds between 1985 and 1995.[29]

Cancer is also linked to our life choices. "Tobacco use, poor diet, and inadequate physical activity combined are related to about 60 percent of all cancer cases, while environmental cancer risks are related to only about 3 percent of cancer cases," reports Dr. J. Nick Baird, director of the Ohio Department of Health.[30]

Factors That Influence Longevity

Would you, with me, prefer to stay a bit longer on this earth? Would you like to find greater energy, joy, and fulfillment in this life? Consider these six factors:

1. Attitude: In recent years numerous scientific studies have shown a positive link between faith and longevity.[31] One study, for example, showed that people who pray accelerate their recovery rate.[32]

On the other side, fuming at other drivers or stewing about the boss will shorten your life.[33] Stress has a strong, negative impact on your longevity. It makes your cells deteriorate faster. Its impact shows up on your skin and in your hair. Have you noticed how quickly a new president grays once he moves into the Oval Office? Nutrition and exercise play an important role in the management of stress, but so does your attitude.

2. Relationships: People with healthy relationships tend to live more satisfying lives. Even pets can have a positive impact on the health of those who live alone.

3. Genes: Diet can make a difference in the fight against our genetic predispositions. For those of us who are genetically predisposed to prostate cancer, eating more soy, more fresh fruits and certain vegetables, and less saturated fat will decrease the risk.[34]

Diet may also have an impact on the genes linked to heart disease, colon cancer, and Alzheimer's.[35] There is a strong link between genetics and the impact of nutrition.

4. Mental activity: Some parts of the brain will keep growing if they get enough exercise.[36] As we get older, it is important to keep learning new things and trying new activities. As I'm using a computer for the first time to write a book, every chapter gets a little better. On the first two chapters, my grammatical challenges were obvious. There were all kinds of squiggly lines under my words indicating numerous misspellings. By the third chapter I'd discovered spell check! I continue to learn new things, and it's creating new pathways in my brain.

5. Exercise and **6. Diet:** The impact of these last two factors on a person's overall well-being cannot be overemphasized. No one wants the debilitation of diabetes; exercise and diet can help keep its risk at bay. The current number-one cause of death in America is heart disease, but it is largely preventable. You can reduce the risk simply by exercising, eating well, and not smoking.

Not long ago I would go home after worship on Saturday nights, fix a big plate of nachos with all the works, and call it dinner! I was ignorant in regard to healthy nutrition. Part of my conversion process was the realization that loss of momentum is based in lifestyle. It's why so many people become ineffective in their sixties. They are spiritually, emotionally, and physically tired, so they simply drop off the path of ascent and retire. I don't know about you, but I'm not going to take myself out of God's game because of poor eating and exercise habits.

The Responsibility of Leadership

As I have emphasized throughout this book, all leadership begins with self-leadership. My influence as a leader comes down to the credibility of my witness to others. Do I demonstrate (w)holiness? Is the lifestyle of Jesus being revealed in my body, mind, *and* spirit? Am I growing continually in my fitness to serve the God whose salvation includes wellness? (John Wesley called this lifestyle emphasis, "Going on to perfection."[37])

It is impossible to effectively lead others if I cannot first lead myself. I must be on the ascent of health holiness if I am to be a healthy, positive, contagious force in the life of others!

> *Do you not know that in a race all the runners run, but only one gets the prize? Run in such a way as to get the prize. Everyone who competes in the games goes into strict training. They do it to get a crown that will not last; but we do it to get a crown that will last forever. Therefore I do not run like someone running aimlessly; I do not fight like a boxer beating the air. No, I strike a blow to my body and make it my slave so that after I have preached to others, I myself will not be disqualified for the prize.* (1Cor. 9:24-27)

It all comes down to the commitment of a rigorous daily discipline. This is why we are called disciples. Discipline is painful for the moment in which it is practiced. Many of Jesus' followers left the journey of ascent because they didn't want to pay the ongoing price of discipleship (see John 6:66). But those who continue on the incline of discipline will celebrate the blessings of God's promise. "*No discipline seems pleasant at the time, but painful. Later on, however, it produces a harvest of righteousness and peace for those who have been trained by it*" (Heb. 12:11).

I must be on the ascent of health holiness if I am to be a healthy, positive, contagious force in the life of others.

Consider the temptation of Jesus in the wilderness. Satan's first attack against Jesus was an attempt to get Jesus to submit his mind and spirit to his appetite. After Jesus fasted for forty days, the tempter suggested that Jesus' comfort and relief would come from food. "*If you are the Son of God, tell this stone to become bread*" (Luke 4:3). Jesus had the mental, spiritual, and emotional discipline to turn Satan down.

Likewise, your daily devotion—your reflective time with God—is the foundation for all disciplines in your life. Your ability to have authority (or discipline) over your physical body is the doorway to all other disciplines in your life.

King David lost his integrity when he surrendered to the passions of his appetite. Instead of leading his men in battle—where leaders are supposed to be—he succumbed to his lust for a married woman (see 2 Sam. 11:1-5). What sets humans apart from all other created species is our ability to master physical discipline, to be able to live by the authority of God's Word and power of the Spirit, not the immediacy of our appetites. Until we are able to exercise discipline over our bodies through the power of the Holy Spirit, our minds and spirits will continue to be held hostage to our appetites and passions.

> **Until we are able to exercise discipline over our bodies through the power of the Holy Spirit, our minds and spirits will be held hostage to our appetites and passions.**

Everyone in America is dealing with exponential increases in the cost of health care insurance. Employers are having to make painful decisions on important benefits that many of us assumed were guaranteed rights, and we must blame ourselves for some of those high costs. Many of us have driven up the price of care by our inattention to personal physical health. Ordained ministers of churches are some of the worst offenders! The West Ohio United Methodist Conference Treasurer says, "We spent more on medications for depression, cardiovascular disease, and sour stomachs than we did for conference benevolences."[38] In others words we spend more on clergy health care than we do on mission! All leadership begins with self-leadership. You can't lead others until you can lead yourself, including the disciplines of managing your physical health, lengthening your leadership.

Lengthening Your Leadership

Would you rather be a short-term leader or one who continues to influence others year after year? Nelson Mandela, the great South African leader, still lives a fruitful life of contribution as he nears his ninetieth birthday. He is spending most of his energies in the fight against AIDS. How does he continue to live faithfully and fruitfully well past eighty? It began with a practice at an early age. According to some reports, in the 1940s Mandela began the disciplined eating and exercise regime of an athlete. I read that he still gets up today by 4:30 AM and begins an exercise routine by 5:00 AM that lasts at least an hour. He reads the daily papers over breakfast at 6:30 and then puts in a standard working day of twelve hours.

John Wesley was still riding the circuit, taking the good news by horseback into his eighties. He would preach in up to three or four places a day.

I had the privilege of attending Asbury Theological Seminary in the 1970s. Julian C. McPheeters, the school's second president, was in his eighties at that time. He was retired but still very active in the seminary community. When you heard him preach, heaven came down! I heard that he learned to water ski in his seventies and that he was still doing aerobic exercise and working with weights in his eighties. He physically outpaced many of us who were still in our twenties! Howard Snyder makes memorable note of this man of God, saying, "Deeply committed to holistic evangelism, McPheeters was instrumental in the integration of nutrition, exercise, physical healing, and social justice, especially racial justice, into the Asbury Seminary curriculum."[39] Dr. McPheeters understood the concept that all leadership begins with self-leadership.

You cannot be a healthy influencer and agent of kingdom change if you are not demonstrating the reality of the kingdom of God within yourself.

You cannot be a healthy influencer and agent of kingdom change if you are not demonstrating the reality of the kingdom of God within yourself. *"You are the salt of the earth. But if the salt loses its saltiness, how can it be made salty again? It is no longer good for anything, except to be thrown out and trampled underfoot"* (Matt. 5:13).

Balanced leadership also includes the responsibility of leading children. I have already mentioned the growing crisis of obesity among our kids. This problem can largely be attributed to a fast-food dependence, a result of busy lifestyles and single-parent or dual-career households. How many of us as parents turn to McDonald's after a hard day at work because it is cheap and easy? Morgan Spurlock's 2004 documentary *Super Size Me* was a wake-up call for a fast-food-dependent nation. Mr. Spurlock ate nothing but McDonald's food three times a day for one month. His body began a rapid descent of deterioration, exhibiting accelerated weight gain and dangerous increases in liver enzymes.

Fast is easy. Discipline is hard!

Another factor is the way today's children live more sedentary lifestyles. When I was a kid, we played outside. "Mom, let me in!" I'd call. But I wasn't allowed to come back in. "I'm cold!" I'd whine. My mother told me to run around to warm up. "Mom, I'm thirsty," I'd try. She reminded me to take a sip from the garden hose. Sometimes she'd bring us a snack like an apple, which we'd eat outside.

We weren't readily allowed back indoors. Mom's babysitter was the outdoors, not the television. When you have to play outdoors, you invent things to do. You are active. You are creative.

It was a lot healthier than watching television, playing video games, and eating junk food.

It blows me away that people are suing fast food companies over their own discipline issues. We need to take responsibility for our own lives.

Beginning Point

Ready for a life of better eating and exercise? If you are like me, you have no idea where to begin, and you need a conversion-level experience to push you to a point where you actually take meaningful action. My head had listened for years to statements about the importance of healthy eating and exercise. My responses had ranged from "Some day I'll get to it" to "I know a lot of people who are worse off than me."

My rationalization proved dangerous. The dinner hour of Friday, August 18, 2000 found me in a Cincinnati restaurant celebrating a family birthday, when I suddenly felt faint. Next thing I remember, paramedics were shoving aspirin into my mouth and I was being rushed by ambulance to a nearby hospital. After a battery of tests in the next days, my doctor determined that the arrhythmia my heart had exhibited was not the indication of a diseased heart but rather the red flag of a huge wake up call. My 911 experience was precipitated by the culmination of lifestyle stress, too much caffeine, and a total disregard for physical conditioning in the journey of ascent.

I knew I had to change if I wanted longevity in ministry, future anniversaries to celebrate with Carolyn, and the joy of grandchildren. My conversion had begun!

A few weeks after my heart scare, I shared during a weekend message how I intended to take charge of this neglected area of my life. I forecasted that I would begin a fitness program, but needed a trainer to show me how.

Chastity Layne Slone approached me after our final worship celebration and introduced herself as a certified trainer. She told me that she would be willing to work with Carolyn and me. We talked about it at home, and a month later set up our first appointment with Chastity. Her first question, as with everyone she trains, was whether we had clearance from our physician. "Filling out a basic health-history evaluation at a fitness club is not enough," she says.

It really helped that we committed as a family to become healthy together. It is a blessing to agree together about keeping certain unhealthy foods out of the house. It is also encouraging to grow together with your children in this area. All five members of the extended Slaughter family (husband, wife, daughter, son-in-law, son) now work out on a regular basis and have become informed about healthy nutrition practices.

Fitness begins with a change of mind. Why am I willing to sweat and hurt? Because it's not about me. My life is not my own. "*For me to live is Christ*" (Phil 1:21)! What's more, my life patterns will be inherited by the generations that follow me.

Fitness Starts with Good Nutrition: Triangle Leg #1

I am not particularly fond of the fad diets where you deprive yourself of certain foods for a period of time. Instead, I learned a plan of nutrition that Carolyn and I could practice for life. "To make diet changes work where you see success, it must be a family decision," says Chastity, our trainer. "If the family chef tries to offer two kinds of food, you'll reinforce the idea that nutritious food is weird, and it will lead to failure." (View "Shopping with Carolyn" video at www.ginghamsburg.org/mfl.)

Chastity should know. She started her fitness journey long before Carolyn and I wised up. She even competes in body-building events and has won some titles. And she too had an accountability partner in her spouse. "I haven't always felt good about what I eat," she says. "It took an eight-year journey, but I don't crave soda pop the way I used to."

Chastity started at a specific point, as Carolyn and I did, where she determined that her eating and exercise habits would change. She then began to make a long series of firm decisions. "The biggest thing I see with failure is someone who never truly made a mind change," she says. "One of the reasons people give up is that there are so many choices for your food, and that's why the decision to change is so important."

Chastity also notes that people have a higher failure rate if they don't work with a professional who can develop a plan. This could be a certified trainer like her, or perhaps someone with training and passion in exercise science, such as a physical therapist. "Without help from someone knowledgeable," she says, "you will hit a plateau, and you'll think that's the best you're going to accomplish."

Though Chastity is a trainer who operates her own fitness center, she has emphasized diet just as much as exercise. One of the first questions she asked Carolyn and me was, "What are you eating?" She wanted to help us calculate how many calories we were taking in and what kinds of foods we were eating. Some people, such as those who eat irregularly and snack a lot, need to journal in order to determine what they actually take in on a typical day.

In recent years, I've come to follow a healthy, balanced diet that is low in fat and is conscious of the daily intake of carbohydrates. I'm learning to distinguish the healthier complex carbs from simple carbs that too quickly turn to sugar. I follow the simple rule, "if it's white, it's not right," and opt for whole grains. These include:

- Wild or brown rice over white rice,
- Whole-wheat bread over white bread,
- Yams over white potatoes, and
- Whole-wheat pasta over white pasta.

Vegetables and fruits are a great way to take in healthy carbs, and again I've learned another general rule of thumb: "The brighter the color of the fruit or vegetable, the higher the value in vitamins and minerals."

I've started to study food packaging in order to pay attention to my daily intake of sugar. Many items state in bold letters on the package that they are "0% fat," but they are loaded with sugar. I have another simple rule: "Don't count daily calories; instead, pay attention to my intake of fats, carbohydrates, and sugar."

I stay away from dessert except on rare, planned occasions.

My eating frequency has also changed. I never used to eat breakfast, but now I realize that breakfast is one of the most important meals of the day. Breakfast kicks in your metabolism, and it is your metabolism that burns fat.

With so many mini-meals, all nutritious, I never feel deprived. I now eat three healthy, balanced meals each day, and I supplement these meals with at least two or three smaller healthy snacks. With so many mini-meals, all nutritious, I never feel deprived.

Another Mike maxim: "Stay away from high-fat and high-sugar snack foods." (They will literally kill me!) Almonds and unsalted peanuts are some of my favorite snacks. I will also eat a granola bar or drink a protein supplement for one of my snacks, usually before or after a workout.

Protein is very important for muscle growth. Lean beef, chicken breast, turkey, and fish are excellent sources of protein that are also low in fat. Egg whites and beans are healthy sources for protein. I stay away from fried and breaded foods.

I drink skim milk, and I drink plenty of water every day. For most people, depending on their physician's advice, it is a good idea to supplement their daily diet with a good multivitamin.

If I ever slip in my eating habits, Chastity reminds me that healthy nutrition is 80 percent of the equation in physical fitness. At first, all I could think about was the new foods I don't especially like or the foods I have to give up. "I can't live without dessert," I'd think.

Then I would remember why I'm making the change: it's not about my likes and food preferences, but the mission of the One I serve!

It's not about my likes and food preferences, but the mission of the One I serve!

Aerobic Exercise: Triangle Leg #2

Aerobic exercise is intentional physical movement that keeps my heart rate up for twenty to thirty minutes. The focus of aerobic exercise is cardio or heart health.

It is important to do some form of cardio exercise at least three times a week. Many choose to have a daily regimen of walking. This is good. I walk to as many places as possible and avoid elevators in favor of steps whenever possible.

Earlier I described the first time Chastity took me out to run for twenty minutes nonstop. I thought I would die! "I've got to stop," I wheezed after just a matter of one minute that seemed like ten. "I'm going to die!"

Chastity promised me that it would get better, and it did within a matter of weeks. Today my aerobic exercise of choice is running three to four times a week on the treadmill. It's easier on my knees and is not affected by the Ohio weather.

The Christmas after we started our commitment to fitness, Carolyn and I bought each other a treadmill for about $800, and it is still serving us well after four-plus years. In fact, before beginning the next section, I will take a break from writing to do a thirty-minute run on the treadmill. See you later!

Resistance Training: Triangle Leg #3

I'm back after running three miles. It is hard to believe that I can physically do more in my fifties than I could when I was in my twenties.

The third part of the fitness triangle is creating resistance with weights. Your muscles are the furnace of your metabolism. Muscle burns fat twenty-four hours a day, seven days a week, even while you sleep. Aerobic exercise burns fat mainly during the time of the exercise, while the heart rate is increased.

I think of it this way: "Aerobic exercise makes for heart health while weight training increases physical strength." I try to do three cardio sessions a week and four weight-training sessions. In each of the four weight sessions, I concentrate on different parts of my body. This means I hit each major muscle area once a week.

I am not trying to look like Arnold Schwarzenegger; my goal is to maintain positive momentum for life. On Monday I concentrate on weight machines and free weights that work my chest and back muscles. On Tuesday morning I will do a half hour of cardio exercise on the treadmill. On Wednesday afternoon I come back to resistance training, by concentrating on leg exercises. On Thursday morning I am back to cardio, by running twenty-five to thirty minutes on the treadmill. On Friday morning I spend twenty-two to twenty-five minutes on the treadmill in my basement and then hit the gym on the way home from the office, in order to work my shoulder muscles (thus a double session on Friday). On Saturday morning I am back at the gym to work my triceps and biceps. Sunday is my day of rest.

Notice that I did three cardio and four weight training sessions that targeted all of my major muscle groups. The best way to really learn to exercise with a safe, healthy routine is to become part of a gym or YMCA where they have classes and trainers who know what they are doing and can teach you to use the right form that will minimize the possibility of injury and maximize the effectiveness of your time spent in the gym.

Good nutrition is 80 percent of the key to your desired results.

Good nutrition is 80 percent of the key to your desired results because food is the fuel that runs the car. My body was not designed to run on inferior fuel!

Conversion Time

Rob, a pastor in his early thirties, began visiting Ginghamsburg's Web site each week, going especially to the online sermons. In January and February 2002, I did a multiple-week series on D-R-I-V-E, which he saw in video stream.

"This message really spoke to me," he told us, "because in December 2003 my blood pressure went so high I had to be rushed to the emergency room. They thought I was going to have a stroke. I was diagnosed with fatty liver, high cholesterol, and high triglycerides. I was a walking, talking stroke or heart attack waiting to happen."

Rob was thirty-one years old, but you wouldn't guess it. "At my highest point, I got up to about 292 pounds," he confessed to us. "My asthma was starting to affect my ability to preach three services. I couldn't stay awake. I was mad all the time. I lost a lot of self-esteem in terms of when I went to places, all I could think about was how people were looking at me and thinking about how fat I was."

Rob began to deal with the issue that his body is a temple of the Holy Spirit. He felt that God was speaking to him and saying, "You need to get your health under control." Rob had a conversion.

He sensed that God was saying, "Rob, if you do this, you are going to lose weight." Today he exercises anywhere from thirty minutes to an hour-and-a-half, depending upon the day and the intensity of the workout. His back pains, developed because of weight gain, have lessened. He's had accountability help from Weight Watchers.

"I had to re-learn how to eat," he says.

Today he has dropped from a high of 295 pounds to about 185. "I feel 100 percent better," he says. "I believe I've pleased God by taking care of my temple. God has taken care of all my medical problems. I believe God has blessed me because I decided to dedicate my temple to him and stop abusing it." (View Rob's story at www.ginghamsburg.org/mfl.)

All leadership begins with self-leadership. Your body is not your own. We are called to honor God with our body. Until we exercise discipline over our bodies, our minds and spirits will be held hostage to our passions and appetites.

Your life is a gift; your body is God's temple. Make your life and body an honorable, excellent offering to God through the discipline of healthy eating and exercise. Have you had *your* conversion?

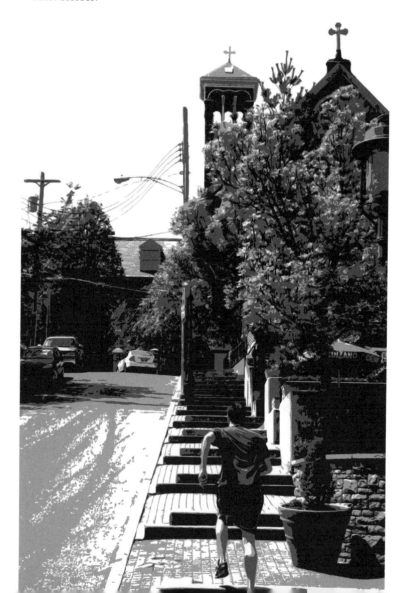

Momentum for Life Devotional

Read aloud the main Scripture, Psalm 128.

1. While we all enjoy the gift of life, some may view a healthy lifestyle as optional. I'd consider adopting a healthy eating and exercise regimen for:
   • overall wellness
   • increased length of life
   • improved physical appearance
   • God's honor

2. This chapter names six factors affecting longevity. Where do you need to start?
   • attitude
   • mental activity
   • relationships
   • exercise
   • genes
   • diet

3. All leadership begins with self-leadership. What are positive and negative ways you've influenced people closest to you in regard to healthy lifestyle issues?

4. Share with someone else what God is saying to you.

CHAPTER SEVEN

Work Your Program: Thriving in Life, Leadership, and Mission

"With you there is forgiveness, so that we can, with reverence, serve you." (Ps. 130:4)

Followers of Jesus are on a lifelong ascent called transformation. Most people, however, come to church seeking relief rather than transformation. The majority are not prepared for the pain and exertion that accompany genuine life change. They choose not to look inside themselves for what God wants to change. It's easier to find an excuse and blame something or someone for whatever is wrong about life. Most prefer to mask pain instead of face it, and humans will reach for work, entertainment, sex, chemicals, sports, people, and even religion to design the mask.

The root of all brokenness is self-absorption, the trap of presuming that "it's all about me." Self becomes the center of our reality. We search

We abandon the path of ascent to go after gods that promise to make us happy. These false gods cannot satisfy the deep longing of our hearts.

for meaning through the pursuit of happiness. We abandon the path of ascent to go after gods that promise to make us happy: toys, entertainment, or other stimulation, but to no avail. These false gods cannot satisfy the deep longing of our hearts.

Prepare for Re-Entry

I remember watching the Columbia space shuttle shatter apart as it re-entered the Earth's atmosphere across the skies of Texas. In the follow-up investigation it was discovered that Mission Control had been aware that a small piece of the aircraft had broken off during takeoff. They saw it, however, as only a minor flaw that would create no real problems. They grew even more confident in the days after launch, as the shuttle circled the earth and showed no further problems.

It was a false confidence.

The shuttle disaster is a metaphor for our personal life. We're vaguely aware of small pieces of brokenness in our innermost being, but we live most of our days in denial, relying on our own resourcefulness. We can look good on the outside, but we have a false confidence. Re-entry is coming, and the end result of destruction—physical, emotional, or spiritual—is a very real possibility. For leaders, the end result is not only self-destructive, but it can also prove devastating to those within our networks of influence.

Time to Repent

The consequence of self-focus is self-reliance. "I can do it," we say. "I'm strong. I can change. I'll find momentum. I can achieve, acquire, and ascend, and I can do it all by myself." We believe in God and profess Jesus, but we live in denial of our need. Our illusion is that the good life is something we can attain for ourselves and by ourselves.

> **Our illusion is that the good life is something we can attain for ourselves and by ourselves.**

How many of us have learned to separate the spiritual part of our lives from our daily work routines? We might explore devotional thoughts every morning before going to work but live the rest of the day in reliance upon self and our own resourcefulness. The only time we need God to help is when we get into a sticky place or a tough spot. We go through our days hardly giving God a second thought. We sing "Amazing Grace," but we don't realize our own great need for amazing grace. "I can do it on my own," we claim. "I can change any time I want. Knowing what is right enables me to do what is right."

When I am in a hurry to get someplace, I'll push the pedal until I'm flying along at up to eighty miles an hour. I drive differently when a police car is behind me. I'm careful, and I watch my mirrors. I look ahead, and if there is a bend in the road, I will slow up a little bit.

My motive is not to do what is right; my motive is to avoid getting a ticket. Why? I'm broken. Something in me knows what is right, but I can't do it, and even when I do manage to do right, my motives are wrong. That's why I need a Savior. True transformation requires a cross.

True transformation requires a cross.

Name Your Junk

Anyone who has been in a twelve-step program knows that the first step in recovery is to become aware of your brokenness and powerlessness. The first Beatitude says. "*Blessed are the poor in spirit, for theirs is the kingdom of heaven*" (Matt. 5:3). Following Jesus involves self-renunciation: admitting, "I am broken." It's the first step towards transformation.

We all must deal with the junk piles that accumulate around our busy lifestyles. They're like the piles in our homes, made up of everything we don't have time to deal with in the activities of daily life. We try to make the piles look pretty, cover them up, or move them from place to place, but it doesn't work. Eventually we must deal with our junk.

Our hearts are the dwelling place of Christ. Jesus and junk cannot share the same space; light and darkness cannot coexist. We dare not rationalize or procrastinate. We must admit our brokenness, acknowledging our sin before God. We cannot let any area of our hearts go unexposed; we must name our junk.

In Luke 15 Jesus tells the story of the awakening of the prodigal son. He is out there, self-reliant and self-sufficient. He loves his father, but he is disconnected from home. *"When he came to his senses, he said, 'How many of my father's hired servants have food to spare, and here I am starving to death.' I will set out and go back to my father"* (Luke 15:17-18).

When the prodigal son realizes his brokenness, he repents and names his junk. *"I will...say to him, 'Father, I have sinned against heaven and against you. I am no longer worthy to be called your son; make me like one of your hired servants'"* (Luke 15:18-19). The son's brokenness informed his new identity: grateful servant. He represents a movement from self to servant.

Receive God's Forgiveness

Even before the prodigal son named his junk, the Father was waiting with open arms. *"So he got up and went to his father. But while he was still a long way off, his father saw him and was filled with compassion for him; he ran to his son, threw his arms around him and kissed him"* (Luke 15:20).

The second step of transformation is to receive God's forgiveness and mercy. *"If we confess our sins, he is faithful and just and will forgive*

Be merciful to yourself and receive God's forgiveness. *us our sins and purify us from all unrighteousness"* (1 John 1:9). We are not in the Father's embrace because we deserve to be here or because we earned our way; we are here because of the cross. Be merciful to yourself and receive God's forgiveness.

Work Your Program

To move forward on the ascent, we must take intentional, disciplined steps every single day. At Ginghamsburg we started a worship celebration for people on the road to recovery. I marvel at the courage and intensity of those who are seeking to radically change their lives. Once controlled entirely by their addiction, these Jesus-followers have named a set of daily practices that they absolutely must carry out in order to survive and thrive. It's their program of recovery, disciplines they work on every day to assure that true change takes place.

You and I are no different. Each of us needs a program of recovery, a personalized combination of life practices that will enable us to build momentum for life, keeping us on an upward climb. When any parts of this program are neglected, we begin to plateau and lose momentum. Worse, we begin to downsize God's dream for our lives.

> **Each of us needs a program of recovery...that will enable us to build momentum for life.**

Your Own Song of Ascent

The practices based on the acronym D-R-I-V-E represent disciplines for sustaining personal health, integrity, and strategic focus as a leader. They are the elements that keep me moving with momentum towards God's promised future.

What will it take for you to sustain momentum today, tomorrow, and into the unknown future? If you don't have a program, a model for living, I invite you to use D-R-I-V-E for thirty days. Think of what a day could look like if you could experience <u>d</u>evotion to God and <u>r</u>eadiness for lifelong learning. How would it feel to know you were giving your best towards <u>i</u>nvesting in key relationships, <u>v</u>isioning for the future, and <u>e</u>ating and <u>e</u>xercising for life?

Your path awaits; your ascent is possible. Commit to self-leadership, for you cannot effectively lead others unless you are effectively leading yourself. Momentum for life will be your blessing as you faithfully live inside the disciplines of your program. Go in God's authority as you move forward in renewed personal health, integrity, and strategic focus.

Momentum for Life Devotional

Read aloud the main Scriptures,
Matthew 5:3 and Luke 15:17-20.

1. Is there a junk pile in your house? Where is it?

2. Can you identify potentially cancerous cells in your heart that could multiply and grow if left unchecked?

3. The disease of sin requires each one of us to intentionally "work a program" of recovery to stay pure in heart. The program that I work is:
   • a daily Bible study (such as *Transformation Journal*)
   • a twelve-step recovery program
   • an accountability partner or cell group
   • all the above
   • I don't have a program

4. What are your next steps for further working your program?

Appendix:
Resources to Keep You Growing

Ginghamsburg Resources

Web link: www.ginghamsburgresources.com/mfl

Momentum: Mass in Motion

Video: "The Nick Hoover Story"
Video: "Momentum for Luka"

Devotion to God

Transformation Journal Web link:
www.ginghamsburgresources.com/tj

Readiness for Lifelong Learning

Video: On the Street, "What Are You Learning?"
Designing Worship, Kim Miller (Group Publishing, 2004)
Out on the Edge, Michael Slaughter (Abingdon Press, 1998)

Investing in Key Relationships

Video: Mike Berry/Medway Church, "The Measure of Greatness"
Video: "The Leland Sprecher Story"

Visioning for the Future

Video: "The Sudan Miracle Offering"
Video: "Fast for Famine"

Web site: http://www.fastforfamine.org

Spiritual Entrepreneurs, Michael Slaughter (Abingdon Press, 1995)

Eating and Exercise for Life

Video: "Shopping with Carolyn"
Video: "What Is Your Program?"
Video: Rob Dauber, "The Temple"

More resources from Ginghamsburg...

UnLearning Church, Michael Slaughter (Group Publishing, 2002)
Real Followers, Michael Slaughter (Abingdon Press, 1999)
Handbook for Multisensory Worship, Volume 1, Kim Miller (Abingdon Press, 1999)
Handbook for Multisensory Worship, Volume 2, Kim Miller (Abingdon Press, 2001)
Art & Soul Video Series, "Transformational Storytelling," www.ginghamsburgresources.com/as
On the Street Video Series, www.ginghamsburgresources.com/ots

Notes

Chapter One

[1] Steve Watters, "Overcoming Cybersex Addiction" http://www.family.org/married/romance/a0017698.cfm. See also http://internet-filter-review.toptenreviews.com/internet-pornography-statistics.html.

[2] Anne Lamott, *Bird by Bird: Some Instructions on Writing and Life*. (New York: Anchor, 1994), p. 21.

[3] *Bird by Bird*, p. 21.

[4] *Bird by Bird*, p. 28.

[5] http://ginghamsburg.com/tjstart

Chapter Two

[6] See Eugene Peterson, *A Long Obedience in the Same Direction: Discipleship in an Instant Society* (Downers' Grove, IL: Intervarsity Press, 1980).

[7] Peg Tyre, "In Search of Something More," *O (The Oprah magazine)*, January 2005, p. 147.

[8] http://www.barna.org/FlexPage.aspx?Page=BarnaUpdate&BarnaUpdateID=181

[9] http://www.barna.org/FlexPage.aspx?Page=BarnaUpdate&BarnaUpdateID=124.

[10] James Tunstead Burtchaell, *The Dying of the Light: The Disengagement of Colleges and Universities from Their Christian Churches* (Grand Rapids: Eerdmans, 1998), p. 329.

[11] Burtchaell, p. 339.

Chapter Three

[12] Bethany McLean and Peter Elkind, *The Smartest Guys in the Room: The Amazing Rise and Scandalous Fall of Enron* (New York: Portfolio, 2003), p. 3.

[13] McLean, *Smartest*, p. 21.

[14] Gordon MacDonald, *Ordering Your Private World* (Nashville: Thomas Nelson, 1997), p. 103.

[15] Kim Miller, *Designing Worship: Creating and Integrating Powerful God Experiences* (Loveland, CO: Group, 2004), p. 137.

[16] Mark Driscoll, *The Radical Reformission: Reaching Out without Selling Out* (Grand Rapids, MI: Zondervan, 2004), p. 21.

[17] Michael Slaughter, *Out on the Edge: A Wake-Up Call for Church Leaders on the Edge of the Media Reformation* (Nashville, TN: Abingdon, 1998).

[18] *Wall Street Journal*, Monday 11/3/2000, pages R28-R29.

Chapter Four

[19] Thornton Wilder, *Our Town* (HarperPerennial, 1938, 1998), p. 108.

Chapter Five

[20] Michael Slaughter, *Spiritual Entrepreneurs: Six Principles for Risking Renewal* (Nashville: Abingdon, 1995), pp. 109-111, text slightly updated for readability and accuracy.

[21] Walt Kallestad and Kirbyjon Caldwell, *Entrepreneurial Faith: Launching Bold Initiatives to Expand God's Kingdom,* (Waterbrook, 2004), p. 109.

[22] For documentation, do a Google or Yahoo search on these words (without the quote marks): "enough food to feed the world United States." Scholars like Jeffrey Sachs, hailed by *Time* magazine as one of the world's 100 most influential people, argue that all of the world's extreme poverty could be eliminated in our time. See his book, *The End of Poverty: Economic Possibilities for Our Time*, (New York: Penguin, 2005).

[23] Rick Warren, *The Purpose-Driven Life* (Grand Rapids: Zondervan, 2002), p. 17.

Chapter Six

[24] Richard Corliss and Michael D. Lemonick, "How to Live to Be 100," *Time* magazine, August 30, 2004, p. 103.

[25] Corliss and Lemonick, p. 104.

[26] "New Calculation: Obesity Now No. 7 Among Causes of Death," April 5, 2005, www.cnn.com/2005/HEALTH/diet.fitness/04/20/obesity.deaths.ap/index.html

[27] James Swierzbin, "Fighting Obesity in America," *The Berkeley Beacon*, 2/17/05, www.berkeleybeacon.com.

[28] Michael D. Lemonick, "The Year of Obesity," *Time* magazine, December 27, 2004.

[29] "Warning: Obesity is the New Tobacco," *The Australian News*, February 21, 2005.

[30] "Cancer linked to choices," *Dayton Daily News*, December 2, 2004.

[31] Kenneth H. Cooper, *Faith-Based Fitness* (Nashville, Nelson, 1995), p. 3-10.

[32] Cooper, *Faith-Based*, p. 3-10.

[33] Corliss and Lemonick, p. 103.

[34] *Newsweek*, "Health for Life," January 17, 2005, p. 48.

[35] Ibid., p. 48.

[36] Ibid., p. 61.

[37] See sermon 40, "Christian Perfection," in The Works of John Wesley, The Bicentennial Edition on CD-ROM (Nashville: Abingdon Press, 2005).[38] *West Ohio News*; June 25, 2004, p. 11.

[39] Howard A. Snyder, "Holiness in Post Modernity: Holiness and the Five Calls of God," paper presented to the Asbury Theological Seminary community on November 11, 2004.